PETERBOROUGH
TO
NEWARK

featuring Grantham

Vic Mitchell and Keith Smith

MP Middleton Press

Front cover: This is Newark Northgate in about 1960, with class V2 2-6-2 no. 60870 running south. The vans are likely to be full of boxes of fish from Grimsby, for Londoners to enjoy. (Colour-Rail.com)

Back cover: Railway Clearing House map for 1947.

Published April 2015
Revised and reprinted July 2016

ISBN 978 1 908174 72 7

© Middleton Press, 2015

Design Deborah Esher
Typesetting Emma Chapman

Published by
  Middleton Press
  Easebourne Lane
  Midhurst
  West Sussex
  GU29 9AZ
Tel: 01730 813169
Email: info@middletonpress.co.uk
www.middletonpress.co.uk

Printed in the United Kingdom by IJ Graphics, Guildford, Surrey. GU4 7WA

INDEX

ACKNOWLEDGEMENTS

We are very grateful for the assistance received from many of those mentioned in the credits, also to D.Anderson, P.G.Barns, C.L.Caddy, A.Cartright, A.J.Castledine, N.Catford, G.Croughton, R.Darvill, G.Gartside, F.Hornby, S.C.Jenkins, D.K.Jones, N.Langridge, B.Lewis, J.P.McCrickard, B.I.Nathan, A.Neale, C.Pinchbeck, K.Proctor, Mr D. and Dr S.Salter, T.Walsh, R.Yate and in particular our always supportive wives, Barbara Mitchell and Janet Smith.

I. Railway Clearing House map for 1947.

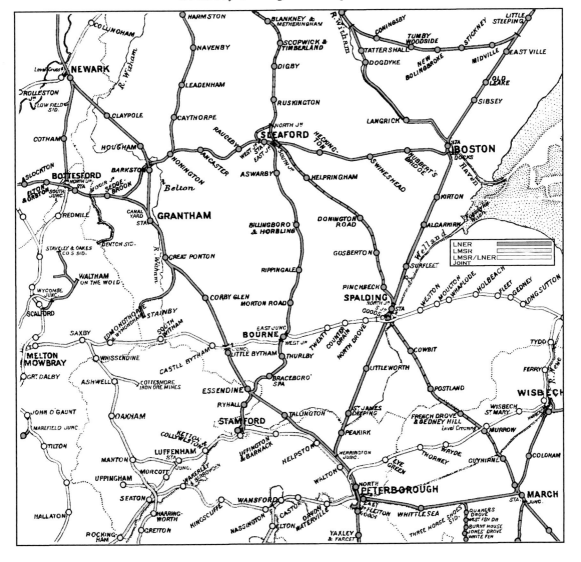

GEOGRAPHICAL SETTING

Peterborough station is a little to the north of the River Nene, over which the main line passes on a massive bridge. The next and much smaller watercourse it traverses is the River Welland, which is just south of Tallington.

A fairly steady climb follows for 15 miles to reach Stoke Tunnel. Here the line passes over a ridge formed of mainly limestone, this linking the Cotswolds with the North York Moors.

The descent is close to the infant River Witham and Grantham is soon reached. The river is within a mile or two of the line as it runs north to Newark. This important market town is on a long bed of red sandstone, parallel to the limestone. The route is on an almost steady descent and this includes Peascliffe Tunnel, after leaving Grantham.

The journey once started in the Soke of Peterborough, which was in Northamptonshire, and soon continued through the eastern extremity of Rutland, at Essendine. The remainder of the route was in Parts of Kesteven in Lincolnshire, the exception being the final three miles, which are in Nottinghamshire.

The maps are to the scale of 25ins to 1 mile and have north at the top unless otherwise stated.

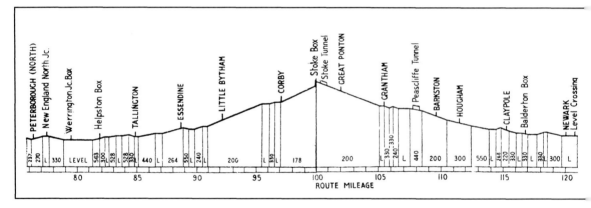

Gradient Profile.

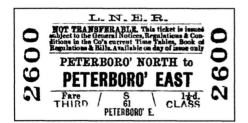

HISTORICAL BACKGROUND

The first line to Peterborough was the London & Birmingham Railway's branch from Blisworth, which opened in 1845. Next, the Midland Railway arrived from Stamford in 1846. The Eastern Counties Railway carried passengers from Ely from 1847.

The Great Northern Railway operated from the south, from Huntingdon and Hitchin, from 7th August 1850. It continued north to Retford from 15th July 1852.

Looking at other connections to the route in geographical order; Grantham was reached from Nottingham in 1850 and from Sleaford in 1857. Newark was served by the MR's Nottingham to Lincoln line in 1846, but the connection came later. Also the Newark to Bottesford branch opened in 1878 and closed in 1987.

A mineral branch was opened in 1917 and it eventually reached Sproxton in 1925. Closure came in 1973. The dates for the intermediate stations and for goods services are in the relevant captions.

Our route became part of the East Coast Main Line (ECML) between London and Edinburgh. The GNR became part of the London & North Eastern Railway in 1923 and the Eastern Region of British Railways upon nationalisation in 1948.

Privatisation resulted in the Great North Eastern Railway Ltd (part of the Sea Containers Group) having a seven year franchise from April 1996; it was extended until November 2007 when National Express took over. In November 2009, Directly Operated Railways used the operating name of East Coast Trains. The subsequent creation of Open Access resulted in the route being used by Grand Central Railway to Sunderland and later by Hull Trains to Hull. The ECML was in public hands for five years until a joint venture involving Stagecoach and Virgin Trains was established in March 2015.

Electrification

The wiring from Huntingdon to Peterborough came into use on 11th May 1987 and the route north to Leeds was electrified on 14th May 1990. The supply was at 25kV AC, by then standard on BR.

PASSENGER SERVICES

The table gives sample figures for down trains running on at least five days per week. The expresses are those stopping at both names in the title of this volume.

	Express		Stopping	
	Weekdays	Sundays	Weekdays	Sundays
1860	5	2	4	1
1880	9	2	4	1
1902	10	3	6	1
1924	4	2	4	0
1955	8	9	6	0
1990	5	4	14	12

The final two figures refer simply to trains calling at Grantham, as all other stations had closed. At all times there were expresses which stopped at only one or neither of the title stations and these are excluded. Many of the wide variety of destinations are revealed in the captions.

London, Peterbro', Nottingham, Retford, Sheffield, Manchester, L'pool, Doncaster, Bradford, Halifax, York, &c.—G. N.

Gen. Man., Seymour Clarke.] [Supt. of Line, F. P. Cockshott.

Miles from King's + G.N.	Fares from King's + (G.N.) 1 cl. s. d.	2 cl. s. d.	3 cls. s. d.	For Metropolitan Line, see page 25.	Week Days 1,2,3 mrn	1,2,3 gov	gov b h	1&2 mrn	1&2 mrn	1&2 mrn	1&2 mrn	1,2,3 mrn	1&2 mrn	1&2 non	1,2,3 p	1&2 aft	1&2 aft	1&2 aft	1&2 aft	1&2 f	1&2 f	Sundays 1,2,3 gov	1&2 aft	1&2 aft	1&2 aft
				Farringdon Street Sta., London ......dep									1057				3 48		4 52	7 48					
	–			,, King's + (G.N.) ,,		6 30	7 40	8 5	9 0	–	10 0	1110	1110	12 0	1 15	2 45	4 0	5 0	5 5	8 0	9 15	7 30	5 0	8 0	–
	0 5	0 3	0 1½	Holloway		6 35		–		10 0										8 5		7 35		8 5	9 15
1½	0 7	0 4	0 2½	Seven Sisters' Road		6 38		–												8 10		7 39		8 10	
2½	0 8	0 5	0 4	Hornsey ....[Park)		6 45														8 15		7 46		8 15	
4	0 9	0 7	0 5	Wood Green (Alexandra		6 48														8 22		7 50		8 22	
5	0 10	0 8	0 6	Colney Hatch		6 53											4 16			8 27		7 55		8 27	
6½	1 4	1 0	0 9	Barnet		7 0		8 25									4 21		5 26	8 36		8 3		8 36	
9½	2 2	1 6	1 0	Potter's Bar		7 9		8 34					–				4 35		n	8 46		8 14		8 46	
12¾	–			Hertford k 86 dep				8 20					1115		1 i20		4 5		5 20	7 40		7 50		6 50	
				Dunstable 86 l ,,				7 55					1049		1250 i		3 40		4 45	7 5				6 15	
				Luton 86 ,,				8 8					11 0		1 i 8		3 56		4 58	7 25		7 35		6 33	
				St Albans 86				8 30					1125		1 30		4 20		4 20	7 55		8 10		5 30	
17¾	3 6	2 3	1 5½	Hatfield		7 20		8 46					1145		1 50	n	4 49		5 46	8 57		8 27		8 57	
22	4 0	3 0	1 10	Welwyn		7 30		8 55							2 0		5 0		5 54	9 10		8 38		9 10	
28½	5 6	4 0	2 4½	Stevenage		7 42		9 7							2 15		5 12		6 6	9 22		8 50		9 22	
32	6 0	4 6	2 8	Hitchin Jnc. [89, 152		8 0	8 40	9 18	–		–		1215		2 30	n	5 25		6 16	9 33		9 2		9 33	
37	7 0	5 0	3 1	Arlesey & Shefford Rd.		8 10			–				1225		2 40		5 35			9 43		9 13		9 43	
41	7 6	5 6	3 5	Biggleswade		8 20		9 33					1235		2 52		5 45		6 35	9 53		9 25		9 53	
44	8 0	6 0	3 8	Sandy 114		8 28		9 38					1242		3 2		5 52		6 42	10 0		9 35		10 0	
47½	8 6	6 6	3 11	Tempsford		8 33							1249				5 59			–		9 41		–	
51¾	9 6	7 0	4 3½	St. Neots for Kimboltn		8 44		9 50					1256		3 15		6 8		6 55	1012		9 50		1012	
55¾	10 0	7 6	4 7½	Offord ....[Ives 93		8 55							1 4		3 25		Stop		j	n		10 2			
58¾	10 6	8 0	4 10½	Huntingdon for St.		9 3	–	10 3					1 25	1 20	3 38				7 10	1025		1013		1025	
69¼	12 6	9 6	5 9	Holme 85		9 22							1 45		3 57				7 26			1031			
				Peterbro' 87. arr		9 40	9 55	1030	1040	1137	1137		2 0	1 50	4 15	4 25		6 40	7 40	1055	11 5	1050	6 40	1055	11 5
76½	13 6	10 6	6 4	Bostn, Grimsby, p 87			1&2						1,2,3												
				113, 93, 153 dep	6 0		10 5		1045	1142	1142		2 10	2 0	4 38	4 30	–	6 45	7 45		1110	11 5	6 45		1110
84½	15 0	11 6	7 0	Tallington	6 15		1022						2 25		4 53				7 57			1120			
88½	15 9	12 0	7 4½	Essendine 83	6 26		1032						2 37		5 3				8 5			1131			
	15 6	11 6	6 10½	92½ Stamford 83, a	6 42		1047						2 55	2 55	5 17	5 17		7 20	8 20			1147			
				153, 116 .... d	6 10		1015	i					2 23		4 45				Stop			1110			
92	16 6	12 6	7 8	Little Bytham	6 35		1042						2 46		5 14							1143			
97	17 0	13 0	8 1	Corby	6 47		1055						2 58		5 25							1155			
102	18 0	13 6	8 6	Great Ponton	g		11 7						3 8		5 35							1210			
105½	19 0	14 0	8 9	Grantham 89, 85	7 11		1123		1130	1227	1227		3 20	2 50	5 50	5 17		7 30	–		12 0	1230	7 30		12 0
	23 0	17 0	10 5	128 Notngham 89 a	8 55		1210		1210	1 30	1 30		4 15	3 30	6 50	6 50		8 5			1240	1 30	8 40		
				See page 89. d	6 5		1015		1015	1140	1140		2 30		5 0	3 50		6 30			1015	1120	6 35		6 35
	22 3	16 3	10 0½	120¾ Sleaford 85 a	8 50		1158		1158				4 0	4 0	8 35	–		8 35				3 52			
				See page 85. d			1040		1040	1040	1040		2 15	2 15				6 40					2 6		
111½	20 0	15 0	9 3	Hougham	7 20		1142						3 31		6 0							1245			
115½	20 6	15 6	9 7	Claypole	g		1150						3 42		6 10	–						1257			
120	21 0	16 0	10 0	Newark 156	7 41		1220		1153				3 58	3 16	6 25	5 38		n				1 20	7 52		
126½	22 6	17 0	10 6	Carlton	7 52		1232						4 11		6 37							1 38			
131¾	23 6	17 6	10 11½	Tuxford ....[173, 172	8 5		1245						4 25		6 49	e						1 55			

LOCAL TRAINS, see page 86.

Gov. as far as York.

3rd class from London at 7 40 mrn to these Stations.

k Cowbridge Station. l Church Street Station.

On Saturdays on

Through Passengers by this Train dine at York.

Through Passengers by this train dine at York.

s Arrive at 4 48 on Saturdays.

e Stop to set down 1st class London Passengers only.

i 3rd class to the North.

n Stop to set down only. j Stops when required.

p 1 & 2 class only from London to Cambridge and Stas. beyond Grantham, Nottingham & Langrick.

3rd cl. fm London to Hull & Scotland, & fm Peterbro', Nottinghm, Grantham, & Retford to Edinbro'.

g Stop by signal to take up, and set down by informing the Guard at preceding station.

3rd cl. fm London to Hull & Scotland, & fm Peterbro', Nottinghm, Grantham, & Retford to Edinbro'.

Noven
1865

LONDON, PETERBRO', NOTTINGHAM, RETFORD, SHEFFIELD, MANCHESTER, L'POOL, DONCASTER, WAKEFIELD, LEEDS, BRADFORD, HALIFAX, YORK, SCOTLAND, &c.—Great Northern.

Gen. Man., H. Oakley.]

From Dover, Canterbury, and Chatham, see page 92. Change at K. C. (G. N.)

Miles from King's Cross	Station		gov mrn	1,2,3 mrn	gov mrn	gov mrn	gov mrn	1,2,3 mrn	1,2,3 mrn	1&2 exp	1,2,3 mrn	1,2,3 aft	1,2,3 mrn	1,2,3 mrn	1,2,3 b	1,2,3 b	1,2,3 mrn	1,2,3 aft	1,2,3 aft	gov aft	1,2,3 aft	1,2,3 aft	1,2,3 aft	1,2,3 aft	1,2,3 aft	1,2,x aft	1,2,x aft	Sundays gov mrn	gov mrn	1,2,3 aft	gov aft	1,2,3 aft
	Victoria								8 4	8b47	8b47		9 15	9 33	1058	1117	1158	1b44	1b44		3 0	3 55	3 55	4 23	5b50	7 25	8g0			3b35	5 35	7 5
	Ludgate Hill								8 36	9b23	9b23		9 50	10 6	11¼b	1151	1233	2b18	2b18		3 56	4 26	4 26	4 56	6b21	8 0	8g33			4b10	6 10	7 40
	Moorgate St.						6 49	7 26	8 30	9 32	9 32		10 1	1016	1138	12 6	1247	2 26	2 26		4 3	4 36	4 36	5 9	6 44	7 48	8 40		8 10	4 35	6 25	8 0
	Aldersgate St.						6 51	7 28	8 32	9 34	9 34		10 3	1018	1140	12 8	1249	2 28	2 28		4 5	4 38	4 38	5 11	6 46	7 50	8 42		8 12	4 37	6 27	8 2
	Farringdon St.						6 53	7 30	8 34	9 36	9 36		10 5	1020	1142	1210	1251	2 30	2 30		4 7	4 40	4 40	5 13	6 48	7 52	8 44		8 14	4 39	6 29	8 4
	King's Crs. (Met.)						6 57	7 34	8 38	9 40	9 40		10 9	1021	1146	1214	1255	2 34	2 34		4 11	4 44	4 44	5 17	6 52	7 56	8 48		8 18	4 43	6 33	8 8
—	King's Cross (G. N.)			5 15			7 15	7 45	9 0	10 0	1010		1035	1040	12 0	1230	1 10	2 45	3 0		4 20	5 0	5 5	5 30	7 0	8 30	9 0		8 35	5 0	6 50	8 20
1¼	Holloway						7 20																						8 40		6 55	
—	Broad Street ....dep						7 8	7 8	8 48				1022	1022	1137		1218		2 42		4 7		4 52	5 13	6 48		8 42				6 33	
2½	Finsbury Park			5 20			7 23	7 52	9 8				1042	1047	12 8		1 18		3 8		4 27		5 13	5 38	7 7		9 7		8 44		7 0	
4	Hornsey ....[Park)						7 28																						8 49		7 5	
5	Wood Green (Alexandra						7 32																						8 53		7 9	
6½	New Southgate & Colny H						7 38																		7 14				8 57		7 14	
8	Oakleigh P., Whetstone						7 44										gov						gov		7 20				9 3		7 20	
9¼	Barnet						7 47							gov			1 29						5 26		7 23				9 7		7 28	
12¾	Potter's Bar						7 57							11 5			1 39								7 32				9 18		7 32	
17¾	Hatfield						8 11	8 28						1117			1 52				4 53		5 48		7 44				9 32		7 44	
22	Welwyn						8 19							1126			2 1						5 51		7 54				9 43		7 53	
28¼	Stevenage						8 30							1137			2 13						6 2		8 5				9 55		8 5	
32	Hitchin		6 5			7 40	8 55	8 44	9 52					1150			2 25			4 0	5 16		6 21		8 15				10 6	5 45	8 16	
35½	Arlesey Siding		6 20			7 48	9 2							1157			2 32			4 7			6 28		8 22				1013		8 23	
37	Arlesey and Shefford Road		6 30			7 52	9 5							12 0			2 35			4 10			6 31		8 25				1017		8 26	
41	Biggleswade		6 45			8 2	9 15							12 9			2 46			4 20	5 30		6 41		8 31				1027		8 33	
44	Sandy Junction 154	gov	6 58			8 20	9 24							1220			2 54			4 26	5 37		6 48		8 41				1036		8 43	
47½	Tempsford	mrn	7 8			8 30	9 31							1227			3 1			Stop			Stop		8 48				1043			
51¾	St. Neots	6 55	7 30			8 40	9 41							1237			3 12				5 49				8 57				1053		8 55	
55¾	Offord & Buckden [214	7 10	7 40			8 49	9 49							1245			3 20			1&2					9 5				11 1			
58¾	Huntingdon, fr St. Ives	7 30	7 55			8 58	9 57	9 20	d					1254		d	3 30			gov	6 1				9 13				1110		9 8	
69½	Holme 133	8 10	8 25				1015							1 12			3 43			aft	6 16				9 30				1128			
76¼	Peterbro' (Priestgt.) a	8 30	8 50	6 48		Stop	1027	9 45	1047		1142		1210	1 25	1 38	2 2	4 0	4 17	4 40		6 27	6 35		7 7	9 43	10 0	1040		1145	6 35	9 35	9 50
	136, 106, 107, 218, d			6 52	5 55		1035	9 50	1052		1147		1215	2 15	1 48	2 7		4 22	4 45	5 0		6 40		7 12		10 4	1049		1153	6 40		9 54
84¾	Tallington ....[155				6 10		1050	10 5						2 30						5 15									12 9			
88¾	Essendine 121			f	6 19		1120	1014	e				f	2 40	2 3		Stop	h		5 25	Stop	f		f					1223			
92¼	Stamford 121 a			7 48	6 37		1157	1037	1157				1248		2 19			4 58		5 48		7 11		7 54								
	(Water Street) d				6 0		11 5	9 30						1 45	1 45					5 6												
92	Little Bytham				6 27		1129		e					2 48						5 33									1231			
97	Corby				6 38		1141	1028	e					2 59						5 44									1245			
102	Great Ponton ....[137				6 4		1151		e					3 9						5 54									1256			
105½	Grantham 119, 136, ar			7 38	6 55		1159	1042	1136	12 9	1229		1256	3 16	2 28	2 49		5 4	5 27	6 1		7 21		7 54		1046	1134		1 4	7 21		1037
130	136 Lincoln (High St. a			8 32	8 32			1233	1233						3 47	3 47						8 53		8 53					5 0			
127½	Nottinghm 119 a			9 6	8 0		1 10	1230	1230		1 10		2 20	4 25	3 35	3 35		5 45	7 15	7 15		8 5		9 0		1130	1 25		2 10	8 45		1 25
	(London Road) d			6 15	6 15		11 5	8 35		11 5	11 5		12 0	2 0		2 0				4 50		6 20		6 55		9 50	9 50		12 0	6 30		8 30
—	Grantham ....dep			7 35	7 0		1235	1047	1139	1216	1232		1 0	3 21	2 33	2 53		5 8	5 30	6 5		7 25		7 57		1049	1139		1 9	7 25		1042
109½	Barkstone				7 8									3 29						6 13									1 16			
111½	Hougham				7 13			l						3 34						6 18									1 21			
115½	Claypole ....[Road)				7 22		1251	Wd						3 43						6 27									1 30			
—	132 Nottingham (London d			7 0					1110						2 5		aft	4 40			aft											
120	Newark 199, 155, 213			7 55	7 34		1 0	11 7	1159					3 54	2 53	Wd	5 16	5 30		6 38	7 50	7 45					12 1		1 42	7 45		k
126¼	Carlton				7 46		1 10	Sat.						4 5			5 26			6 49	8 1								1 53			
131¾	Tuxford				7 57		1 20	Sat.						4 16	i		5 35			7 0	8 12								2 4			
138½	Retford 248 to 250, 213 ar			8 22	8 9		1 31	1135	1227		1 15		1 43	4 28	3 21	3 39	5 45	5 55	6 14	7 12	8 23	8 9		8 41		j	1228		2 17	8 11		1127
183¾	249 Hull (Corp. Pier) arr			1055	1055			2 5					4 55						9 45	9 45	Stop											
162	Sheffield 250 .... ,,			8 58	8 58			1230			1 53			5 48		4 16	6 31	6 31		8 15		8 44				1215	1 10			8 45		
188½	Huddersfield 249 ,,			10 8	10 8			2 7			3 8			7 57		5 36	7 57	7 57		10 6		10 6								1015		
238	L'pool (Central) 245 ,,			1130	1130			3 40			4 25			8 45		6 45	8 45	8 45		1115		1115								11 5		
203½	254 Oldham (Clegg St.) ,,			1115	1115			2 30			3 25			7 53		5 47	7 53	7 53		1030		1030								1040		
211	Rochdale 253 .... ,,			1228	1228	gov		3 18			4 0			8 20		6 22	8 20	8 20		1110		1110										
203	Manchester 251 ,,			10 5	10 5	mrn		2 30			3 10			7 45		5 30	7 45	7 45		9 55		9 55								10 0		

Departures.—Local Trains, p. 122.

Weds. and Sats.

Mondays only.

Mondays only.

Saturdays only, Retford to Doncaster.

Through Passengers by this Train dine at York.

j Passengers not booked to Retford.

k Stops to set down from London or take up for York and Stations North thereof.

Tuesdays only Hitchin to Sandy Junction.

g Change at King's Cross (G.N.) h A Carriage slipped for Stamford & Bourn. i Stop to set down 1st cl. London Passengers only.

Pullman Dining and Drawing Room Saloon Car, King's Cross to Leeds.

e A Carriage slipped at Essendine for these Stations. f A Carriage slipped for Stamford.

Scotch Express.—Pullman and East Coast Sleeping Cars for Scotland.

East Coast Sleeping Car, King's Cross to Edinboro' and Glasgow.

Scotch Express.

b Passengers from Victoria and Ludgate Hill change carriages at Aldersgate street.

c Stops to take up for Leeds.

d A Carriage slipped.

Scotch Express.—Pullman and East Coast Sleeping Cars for Scotland.

April
1880

Down. Week Days.

October 1911

Miles	Station																														
	KING'S CROSS ....dep.																														
	Broad Street "																														
2¼	Finsbury Park "																														
17¼	Hatfield "																														
32	Hitchin "																														
36	Three Counties																														
37	Arlesey and Shefford Road																														
41	Biggleswade																														
44	Sandy 449																														
47¼	Tempsford																														
51	St. Neots																														
55	Offord and Buckden																														
58½	Huntingdon 307, 611																														
63½	Abbott's Ripton																														
72¾	Holme 375																														
76½	Yaxley and Farcet (369																														
100¼	Peterbro'(Cowgate)308,310,a arr.																														
	348 CROMER (Beach) arr.																														
84½	Peterbro' 346, 388, 451, dep.																														
88¾	Tallington ** (452, 605																														
92¾	Essendine 375, 386																														
	386 STAMFORD arr.																														
	(Water Street) dep.																														
92¾	Little Bytham ‡‡																														
97	Corby																														
102	Great Ponton																														
105½	Grantham 380, 382, 390 arr.																														
130	380 LINCOLN (High Street) arr.																														
128¾	382 NOTTINGHAM																														
	385 (Victoria) dep.																														
	Grantham dep.																														
109¼	Barkstone																														
111¼	Hougham																														
115¼	Claypole																														
120	Newark §§ 380, 602, 612 arr.																														
	385 NOTTINGHAM (Vic.) dep.																														
	Newark dep.																														
126½	Carlton-on-Trent																														
127½	Crow Park, for Sutton-on-Trent																														
131¼	Dukeries Junction 672, 673																														
132	Tuxford †																														
138½	Retford 596, 661, 666 arr.																														
146	666 WORKSOP arr.																														
161¼	666 SHEFFIELD (Victoria)																														
287¾	667 STOCKPORT (Tiviot Dale)																														
203	667 MANCHESTER (Lon. Rd)																														
209	667 (Central)																														
202¾	667 LIVERPOOL (Central)																														
	Retford dep.																														
141½	Barnby Moor and Sutton																														
144	Ranskill																														
149½	Scrooby																														
147½	Bawtry ††																														
151½	Rossington (667, 735																														
156	Doncaster 345, 400, 660 arr.																														
196½	735 HULL (Paragon) arr.																														
		1	2	3	4	5	6	7	8	9	10	11	12	13	14	15	16	17	18	19	20	21	22	23	24	25	26	27	28	29	30

Down. Week Days.

July 1924

Miles	Station
	KING'S CROSS ....dep.
	Broad Street "
2¼	Finsbury Park "
17¼	Hatfield "
—	702 CAMBRIDGE ....dep.
32	Hitchin ....dep.
36	Three Counties
37	Arlesey and Shefford Road
41	Biggleswade
44	Sandy 361
47¼	Tempsford
51¼	St. Neots
55¼	Offord and Buckden
58¼	Huntingdon (North) 577, 758
63¼	Abbotts Ripton
69¼	Holme 711 (942
72¼	Yaxley and Farcet (732, 759,
76¼	Peterbro'(N.)363,365,591, ar
107¼	732 BOSTON ....arr.
154¼	734 GRIMSBY TOWN "
160½	942 CROMER (Beach) "
—	759 NEWMARKET ....dep.
—	758 CAMBRIDGE 759 "
—	759 HARWICH (Town) "
—	749 " (Parkeston Quay) "
—	757 IPSWICH "
—	759 YARMOUTH (V.) 943 "
—	759 LOWESTOFT (Cen.) 943 "
—	759 CROMER (G.E.) 943 "
—	759 NORWICH (Thorpe) 943 "
—	Peterbro' (North) ....dep.
84¾	Tallington **
88¾	Essendine 639, 691
92¾	Little Bytham ‡‡
97	Corby
102	Great Ponton
105¾	Grantham 718, 736 ......arr.
128¾	718 NOTTINGHAM (Vic.) ....arr.
130	736 LINCOLN (L. N. E.) "
120½	736 SLEAFORD "
—	Grantham ....dep.
109¼	Barkston
111¼	Hougham
115¼	Claypole
120	Newark §§ 600, 601, 716, 718 {arr. / dep.
126½	Carlton-on-Trent
127½	Crow Park, for Sutton-on-Trent
131¼	Dukeries Junction 823
132	Tuxford (North) †
138½	Retford 809, 814 ....arr.

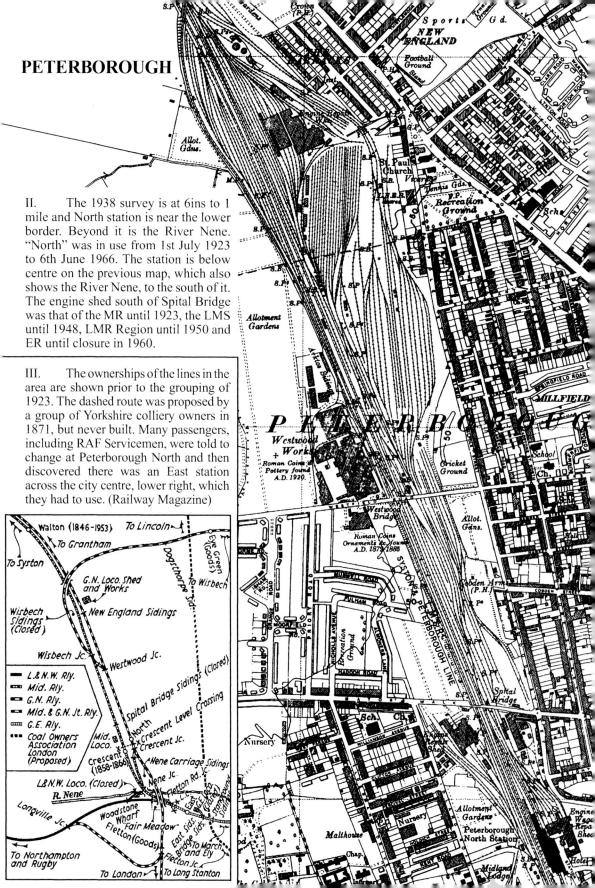

PETERBOROUGH

II.   The 1938 survey is at 6ins to 1 mile and North station is near the lower border. Beyond it is the River Nene. "North" was in use from 1st July 1923 to 6th June 1966. The station is below centre on the previous map, which also shows the River Nene, to the south of it. The engine shed south of Spital Bridge was that of the MR until 1923, the LMS until 1948, LMR Region until 1950 and ER until closure in 1960.

III.   The ownerships of the lines in the area are shown prior to the grouping of 1923. The dashed route was proposed by a group of Yorkshire colliery owners in 1871, but never built. Many passengers, including RAF Servicemen, were told to change at Peterborough North and then discovered there was an East station across the city centre, lower right, which they had to use. (Railway Magazine)

1.   This eastward view was published on 10th August 1850 and features the new GNR bridge over the River Nene and also over the GER. In the background is the cathedral, the building of which was started in the 12th century. (Illustrated London News/Peterborough Museum)

2.   The only entrance was on the east side of the station and is seen on an Edwardian postcard. The ridge of the massive train shed is included, on the left. Centre is the square tower at the end of the footbridge. (P.Laming coll.)

3.   Much of the footbridge was under the main roof and thus users were subjected to overdoses of choking smoke. Another serious problem with this early design was that only two short platforms were provided. (P.Laming coll.)

4.   The west side of the station is evident on the left and the MR's running line is close to it. In the foreground is its coal yard. It had a station called "Crescent" beyond the right border from 1858 to 1866, after which time its trains used "East" station. (P.Laming coll.)

5.   The pointed tower and the flat-top one indicate the extent of the footbridge in this northward view from Crescent Bridge in about the 1930s. It had replaced two level crossings in 1913. On the right is the GNR Hotel, which was the only structure still in use in 2015. It gained fame as the meeting place of the Steam Plough Club. (LOSA)

6.   In the background of this eastward view is St. Peter's Cathedral and on the left is class A4 4-6-2 no. 4900 *Gannet*, in the streamlined form. Also included are nos 6072 and 4407, all facing north. (SLS coll.)

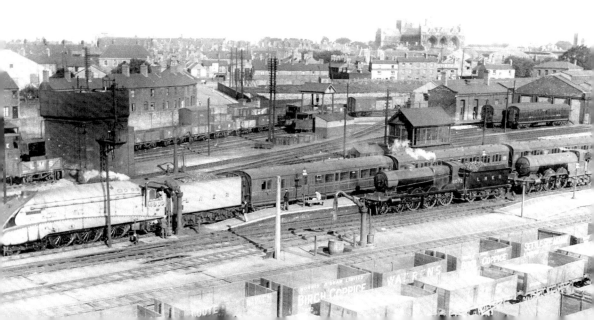

7.	A later northward picture has Spital Bridge in its background and a parcels dock is on the right. The nameboard may be a World War II postwar one, which had replaced a larger one that had occupied the empty frame. North Box is included. (LOSA)

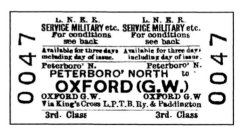

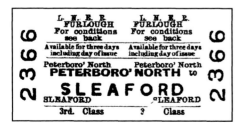

8.	Crescent Road bridge is the background of this better quality view from 1952. "The West Riding" is headed by class A1 4-6-2 no. 60119 *Patrick Stirling*. It is on the down fast line. (P.Kingston)

9.	Looking south in August 1953, we see much of the former GNR Engine & Wagon Repair Shed. There were three foot crossings over which staff carried parcels and mail bags. There was no subway. Around 3500 items were handled each night in 1936, plus 400 boxes of flowers and 3000 crates of fruit in season. (R.M.Casserley)

10.   Seen in 1959 is platform 2 on the right; it had the main entrance and a bay platform (No.1) at the London end. No. 3 had a bay at the other end, numbered 4. Rail Express Parcels and Royal Mail both had their own facilities at New England from 1970 onwards. (Stations UK)

Other views of Peterborough's stations can be seen in Middleton Press albums *Branch Lines around March, Branch Lines around Wisbech, Peterborough to Kings Lynn, Hitchin to Peterborough, Peterborough to Lincoln* **and** *Northampton to Peterborough.*

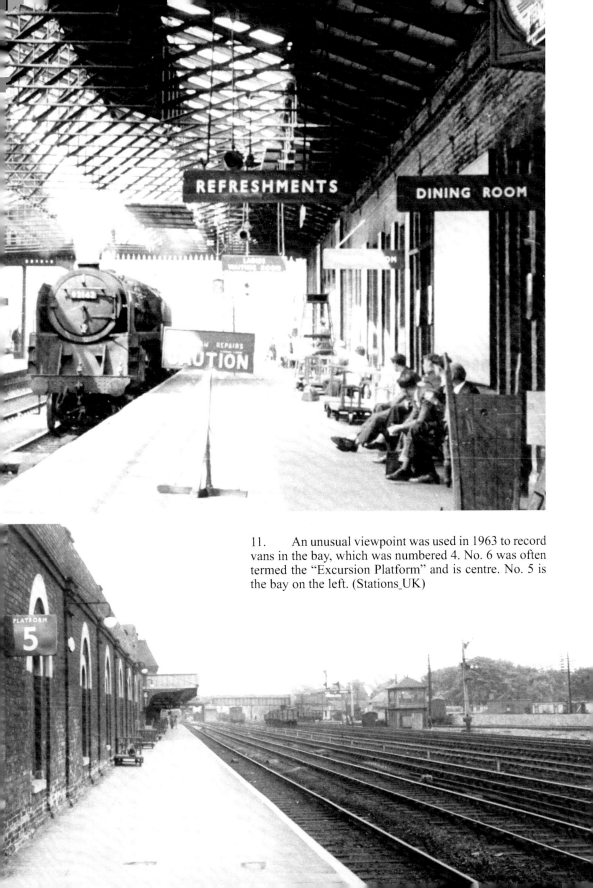

11.   An unusual viewpoint was used in 1963 to record vans in the bay, which was numbered 4. No. 6 was often termed the "Excursion Platform" and is centre. No. 5 is the bay on the left. (Stations_UK)

12.   In conjunction with the colour light resignalling of the ECML through the area, the station tracks were remodelled in 1968-69 to eliminate the previous awkward 'dog-leg' which restricted non-stop trains to 20mph. New 100mph through fast lines were provided, together with a new down island (platforms 4/5) on the west side. Nearest us on 2nd May 1975 is no. 47526, with a train destined for Kings Cross. The up freight train is hauled by no. 45121 and stands at the new platform, which was numbered 4. Diesel locomotives were introduced here in 1958. (T.Heavyside)

13.   A transitional photograph features a DMU devoid of a number and cats whiskers, suggesting that it is one of the first and thus that it is 1955. Ancient structures surround it, including North Box. (Colour-Rail.com)

14.   No. 47476 is hauling the 12.35 Hull to Kings Cross on 4th July 1978. The new footbridge at the rear of the train is for Post Office mail from the adjacent sorting office. On the right of the camera was the bay platform for local trains to Hitchin. (J.Whitehouse)

15.   The 14.00 Kings Cross to Edinburgh is shown on the same day, with no. 254005 leading. The straightened tracks were of great benefit to such HSTs, which ran non-stop here. In the left background is the power station; its fuel came on the River Nene by barge and by rail from 1950. Its ash went to Fletton by rail. (J.Whitehouse)

16.   Looking north in 1969, we see the new through lines and vestiges of the old station on the right. In the sidings on the left are fly ash wagons that would unload at the Fletton worked out brick pits. The ash was mixed with water and filled into the holes to make the site of todays Hampton township. (A.C.Mott)

17.   It is 24th October 2013 and the building of the new platforms is proceeding as part of the station rebuild. The revised speed limit is evident; it had been 20mph for generations. (A.C.Mott)

18.   On 28th December 2013, a new platform 3 serving the ECML up fast through line plus an additional down island (platforms 6/7) on the west side, serving the March lines only, were brought into use. Also on this date the short up bay platform 1 at the south end was abolished and platforms 2 and 3 were both extended and renumbered platforms 1 and 2 respectively. An East Midlands train has just arrived from Grantham. The slopes were to aid Post Office trolleys. (A.C.Mott)

19.   A northward panorama on 9th September 2014 has the new platform for trains to and from March on the left. The extent of the electrified lines is also evident. (A.C.Mott)

NORTH OF PETERBOROUGH

20.   HST no. 254014 is working the 08.10 Edinburgh to Kings Cross on 4th July 1978. HSTs were introduced to the route in March of that year. From that November they ran to Edinburgh, Aberdeen and to Inverness, the latter being one of the longest distance journeys in the country, but not stopping here now. (J.Whitehouse)

21.   No. 55012 *Crepello* heads the 08.05 Kings Cross to Hull on 5th May 1981. In the holding sidings that day were nos 37023, 40092 and 31292. Little was left of the former MR goods yard. (T.Heavyside)

22. Westwood Bridge is in the background of this picture and several others which follow. The main lines of the MR and the GNR both ran under this bridge, with two sidings separating them. The year is 1958. (M.J.Stretton coll.)

23. No. 47572 is pictured at the same location on 4th May 1981, with holding sidings and the fuelling point on the right. The buildings in the background on the far right have been redeveloped into a large retail park occupying the old railway sidings. (T.Heavyside)

24. An up van train is seen on the same day and it is hauled by no. 31013. Resting in the stabling area is no. 31168. (T.Heavyside)

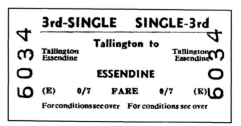

25.   A view north from Westwood Bridge on 1st September 1955 features class W1 4-6-4 no. 60700 *Hush Hush* having suffered a broken bogie frame. New England Yard is on the right and centre is Westwood Junction signal box, which had 60 levers and was in use from 1873 until 21st March 1971. (British Railways)

26.   We are now about a mile from the station and have come to the Eastfield 65-lever signal box. It came into use in 1893 and was still working in 2015. However, it did not control the ECML, only the south end of the yards on the east side of the main line. Peterborough Power Signal Box eventually controlled the route from Sandy to Stoke Tunnel. The photograph is from 11th October 1989. (A.C.Mott)

27.   The ex-GNR New England Sheds can be seen near the top of map II, north of the very extensive New England Yards. The facilities were recorded on 29th August 1960, from the south. The fitting shed is on the left. There were 111 locomotives listed here in 1959. (R.S.Carpenter)

28.   The west part of the shed is seen on 20th May 1938, along with 4-4-2T no. 4505 of class C12, which was produced in 1898-1907. The running shed was coded 35A in 1949-58 and 34E until closure to steam in January 1965. It continued as a diesel depot until 1968. (H.C.Casserley)

29.   The ECML is centre in this southward panorama from the bridge shown in the next picture. The New England Yards and the 1939 water tower are seen on 9th August 1961. New England North Box is on the left and the ex-MR Wisbech West Junction Box is in the right foreground. In the left background is the ex-GNE engine shed. (M.Back)

30.   This is the ex-M&GNR flyover which was demolished during October 1961. The north ends of the siding featured in the previous picture are shown here. (M.Back)

31.   No. 66420 approaches Peterborough station on the up slow line with a Felixstowe-bound Freightliner train on 25th September 2008. On the right is Peterborough Virtual Quarry, with a GB Railfreight class 66 in attendance on an infrastructure train. In the distance are two further GBRF class 66 locomotives - one stabled in the maintenance shed and the other waiting to depart for Felixstowe, after pausing for a crew change. North of here was Walton signal box, from 1875 to 1971, and also Walton station on the Stamford route until 1953. A gate box was provided in 1971 until the crossing was abolished in 1976. (P.D.Shannon)

32.   We are now two miles north of the station where the double track to Spalding branches east. No. 61144 of class B1 passes Werrington Junction Box. It had 70 levers from its opening in 1891 until 7th May 1972 and a panel until closure on 25th February 1973. There were water troughs north of the junction and further north were signal boxes at Helpston, Maxey Crossing, Nunton and Lolham. Only the first was open in 2015. (Colour-Rail.com)

33.   No. 66166 pulls away from a signal check on the up slow line at Marholm with the 13.57 Wakefield-Felixstowe intermodal train on 16th June 2011. The level crossing at this location was closed in December 1995 and a replacement footbridge was provided for pedestrians and cyclists. The reason for the five tracks between Peterborough and Helpston is that the down Stamford line doubles up as the down slow for the East Coast main line. That also explains why the down Stamford line is electrified, whereas the up one is not. (P.D.Shannon)

34.	Helpston station lay on the Midland Railway route just where it diverged from the ECML. It closed to goods in May 1965 and to passengers in June 1966. With Grade II goods shed still standing albeit long devoid of any tracks, no. 37146 crosses over from the ex-MR route to the ECML with the Duxford-Tyne Yard Speedlink train on 21st July 1987. The load includes empty urea hoppers returning from Duxford to Middlesbrough and empty methanol tanks from Duxford to Haverton Hill. (P.D.Shannon)

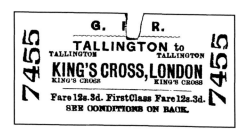

TALLINGTON

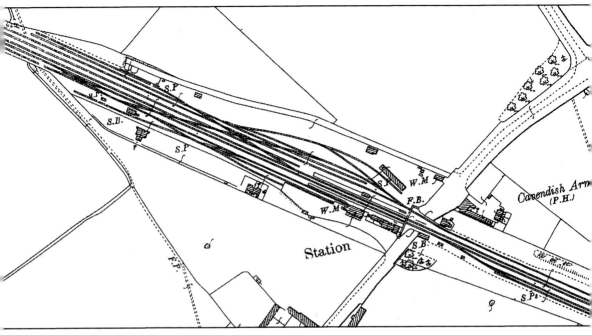

IV.   The 1926 edition includes weighing machines for road vehicles marked W.M. Until 1883, the Earl of Lindsay had the right to stop any train here, except Scottish expresses. There was a 30-cwt crane in the goods shed.

35.   A postcard franked on 8th June 1918 includes the 1874 Tallington South Box, which had 65 levers and was in use until 13th April 1975, when replaced by a small gate box. The suffix was lost in 1926, when the 60-lever Tallington North Box closed. North of it was the 1872 Greatford Box, which lasted until 1975. (P.Laming coll.)

36.   A 1955 panorama has the goods shed centre and the roofless gents to the left of it. Passenger service ceased on 15th June 1959 and goods followed on 7th February 1966. Dow-Mac had a siding on the east side for many years to serve their concrete sleeper works. In April 1981, Redland Aggregates opened a stone terminal, running trains from Mountsorrel, near Leicester. (Stations UK)

37.   Another 1950s panorama and this includes the goods office on the west end of the shed. The single chimney served its stove. The local population was 238 in 1901 and 213 in 1961. (SLS coll.)

38. It is 3rd March 1956 and class V2 2-6-2 no. 60849 runs southwards with a lengthy freight train. Two loading gauges are evident, but the second signal box had gone 30 years earlier. (J.Chesney coll.)

39. A view from around 1965 has the new extra through line on the right. It appears that one gate was moved; lifting barriers worked under CCTV were soon to arrive. Revised running brought two up lines on the left and two down on the right. The new line came into use on 7th August 1960 following the abolition of the down sidings and demolition of the station. (J.Chesney coll.)

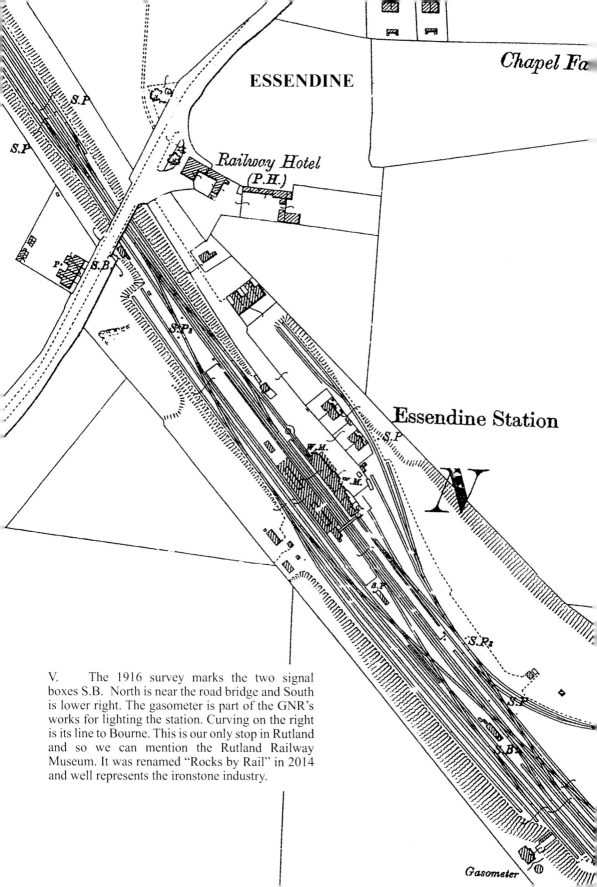

ESSENDINE

Chapel Fa

S.P.

S.P

Railway Hotel
(P.H.)

P. S.B.

S.P.

Essendine Station

S.P

W.H.

M.

N

S.P

S.Ps

S.P.

S.Bx

V.   The 1916 survey marks the two signal boxes S.B. North is near the road bridge and South is lower right. The gasometer is part of the GNR's works for lighting the station. Curving on the right is its line to Bourne. This is our only stop in Rutland and so we can mention the Rutland Railway Museum. It was renamed "Rocks by Rail" in 2014 and well represents the ironstone industry.

Gasometer

40.   The goods yard was provided with a crane rated at 4 tons 18 cwt. This is a southward panorama from the road bridge and includes the staff cottages on the left. (P.Laming coll.)

41.   Class C1 4-4-2 no. 2879 is arriving with the 1.05pm Peterborough to Grantham on 17th April 1947. On the left is one of the GNR's somersault signals. South Box is also in the previous picture. It had 110 levers when closed and was open from 1874 until 21st December 1964. (H.C.Casserley)

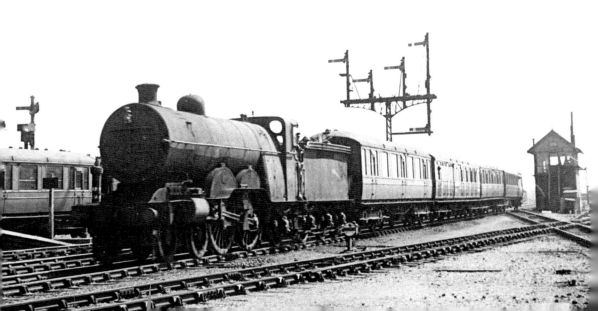

42.　　　Class C12 4-4-2T no. 7368 is seen with the 9.10 to Stamford on 28th August 1947. This line was open from 1856 to 1959. The route northeast to Bourne served from 1860 to 1951 and trains used the up bay. (SLS coll.)

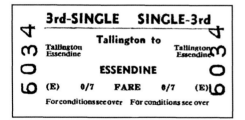

3rd-SINGLE　　SINGLE-3rd

Tallington to

Tallington
Essendine

Tallington
Essendine

ESSENDINE

(E)　0/7　　FARE　　0/7　　(E)

For conditions see over　For conditions see over

6034

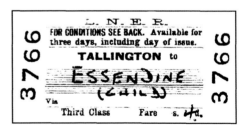

L. N. E. R.

FOR CONDITIONS SEE BACK. Available for three days, including day of issue.

TALLINGTON to

ESSENDINE

(CHILD)

Via

Third Class　　Fare　　s.　d.

3766

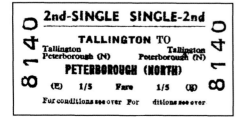

2nd-SINGLE　　SINGLE-2nd

TALLINGTON TO

Tallington
Peterborough (N)

Tallington
Peterborough (N)

PETERBOROUGH (NORTH)

(E)　1/5　　Fare　　1/5　　(E)

For conditions see over　For　ditions see over

8140

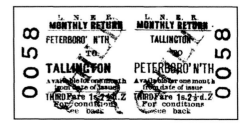

L. N. E. R.
MONTHLY RETURN

PETERBORO' N'TH
TO
TALLINGTON

Available for one month from date of issue

THIRD Fare 1s.2¼d.Z
For conditions
see back

L. N. E. R.
MONTHLY RETURN

TALLINGTON
TO
PETERBORO' N'TH

Available for one month from date of issue

THIRD Fare 1s.2¼d.Z
For conditions
see back

0058

43.　　A 1955 photograph reveals the excellent weather protection provided by the GNR and the helpful sign suffix CHANGE FOR STAMFORD. The number of residents rose from 203 in 1901 to 766 in 1961. (H.C.Casserley)

44.　　The northbound "Yorkshire Pullman" was hauled by class A4 no. 60017 *Silver Fox* on 8th September 1956. It was two miles north of this station that one of this class took the world speed record for steam on 3rd July 1938. No. 4468 *Mallard* reached 125mph and has not been beaten. (N.Sprinks)

45.   Class A3 4-6-2 no. 60056 *Centenary* appears to be working a local train in this record from around 1956. Two of the tracks have lost the old bullhead rail. There was a box called Monkswood north of the station in use from 1898 to 1930. (SLS coll.)

46.   It is 28th May 1956 and we have a fine study of the layout. The cattle pens are on the left and the water tank is on the right, as are two of the columns for filling tenders. (B.W.L.Brooksbank)

47.   Roaring through on 26th September 1958 is no. D201 with the southbound "Tees/Tyne Pullman". The 1Co-Co1 was built that year by English Electric at the Vulcan Foundry and later became class 40. North Box (left) had 55 levers and was worked from 1912 until 13th April 1975. (R.G.Nelson/T.Walsh)

48.   Rattling a loose coupled train at the same location is class K3 2-6-0 no. 61808. Each wagon had just a hand brake lever, a few of which were often left to jump up and down noisily on the journey. (G.Adams/M.J.Stretton)

49.　　The east elevation is shown, plus some of the staff, after the rebuilding. The customary ventilators were not included, but the toilet windows are open wide, instead. (P.Laming coll.)

LITTLE BYTHAM

50.　　This early postcard shows the embankment of the Wymondham - Bourne line on the right. It is beyond the top border of the map. We are looking north, up Station Road, with the station on the left. (P.Laming coll.)

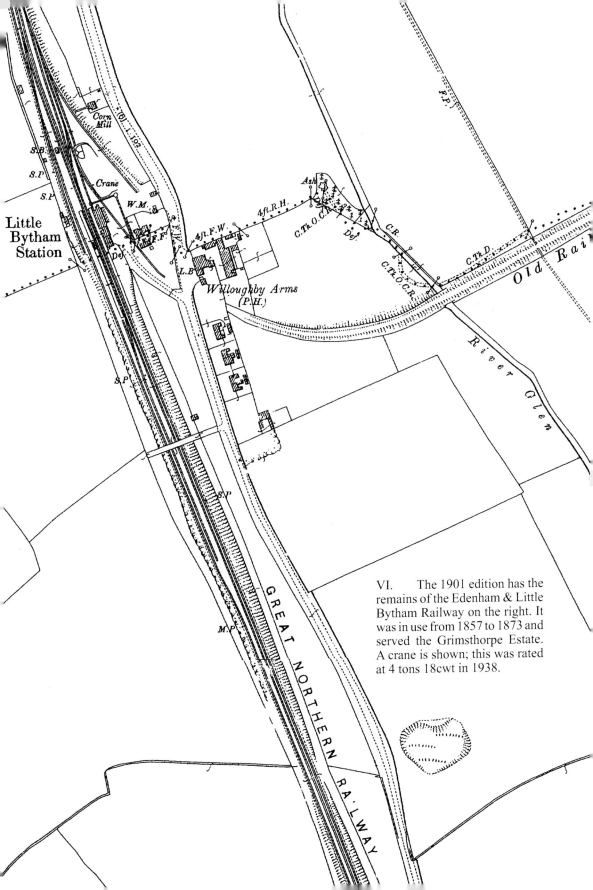

Little
Bytham
Station

Corn
Mill

S.B.

S.P

S.P

Crane

W.M.

Def.

F.F.

L.B.

4ft.F.W.

Willoughby Arms
(P.H.)

S.P

S.P

M.P

GREAT NORTHERN RAILWAY

4ft.R.H.

Ash

C.Tk.O.C.R.

Def.

C.R.

C.Tk.O.C.R.

C.Tk.D

Old Rai

River Glen

F.P.

VI.   The 1901 edition has the
remains of the Edenham & Little
Bytham Railway on the right. It
was in use from 1857 to 1873 and
served the Grimsthorpe Estate.
A crane is shown; this was rated
at 4 tons 18cwt in 1938.

51.   Fine valances and luxury chimney pots add to the status of the structure. The latter were designed to reduce the risk of down draught. (P.Laming coll.)

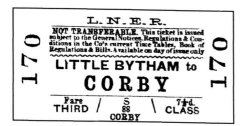

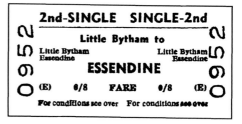

52.   Even a covered footbridge was provided, although the village population was only 378 in 1901. It had just climbed to 481 by 1961. (P.Laming coll.)

53.   Photographed on 13th August 1949 is class A4 no. 60028 *Walter K. Whigham*. The bridge roof had been lost, as has the headboard "The Flying Scotsman". At least the oval lavatory windows are still perfect, having been an LNER feature. (P.H.Wells/SLS)

54.   Bytham Box (no prefix) was opened in 1872 and was the third one here. It had 70 levers and was closed on 6th July 1975. Approaching on 26th September 1958 is class V2 2-6-2 no. 60893, which was not named. The village was half a mile north of the station. (R.G.Nelson/T.Walsh)

55.   A 1959 survey shows desolation. Passenger service was withdrawn on 15th June of that year; freight followed on 1st November 1965. There had earlier been a private siding for Lawnwood Brickworks. It had a signal box from 1879 to 1913 and there were three other boxes further north which closed early. (Stations UK)

EAST OF LITTLE BYTHAM

56.   A relic of the four-mile route to Edenham was found in May 1940. It carried the Witham-on-the-Hill road. The line carried passengers from 8th December 1857 to 17th October 1871 and freight for about two years longer. The route was unprofitable and a buyer could not be found for it by the estate owner. (W.A.Camwell/SLS)

VII.   The 1946 edition at 1ins to 1 mile shows the E&LBR route as a farm track, almost straight. The timetable was published by Bradshaw in December 1871 and shows two return trips, weekdays only.

* Leaves at 3½ aft. on Saturdays. | EDENHAM and LITTLE BYTHAM. [† Leaves at 4 aft. on Saturdays.
From **Edenham** at 10 10 mrn and *4 50 aft. From **Little Bytham** at 12 2 and †5 30 aft. Distance, **4 miles.**
No Sunday Trains. FARES.—1st class, 9d.; 2nd, 6d.; 3rd, 4d. DAY TICKETS.—1st class, 1s.; 2nd, 9d.

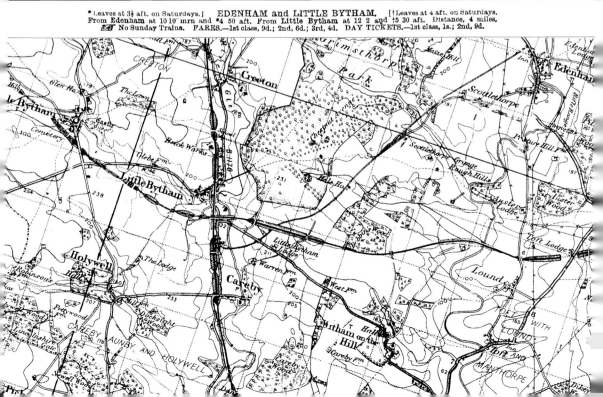

SOUTH OF CORBY GLEN

57.　　No. 47079 *G J Churchward* is hauling a Motorail service near Swayfield on 20th April 1985. There had been an intermediate signal box of that name until 1913. (J.Acton/M.J.Stretton)

EDENHAM and LITTLE BYTHAM.

From **Edenham** at 8 20, 10½, and 11 40 mrn.; 2 25 and 4 55 aft.
mrn.; 12 10, 2 50, and 5 35 aft.　　Distance, 4 miles.　　No Sunday Trains.
FARES.—1st class. 9d.; 2nd, 6d.; 3rd. 4d.　　DAY TICKETS.—1s.: 9d

November 1865

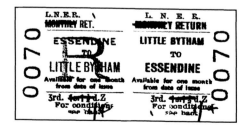

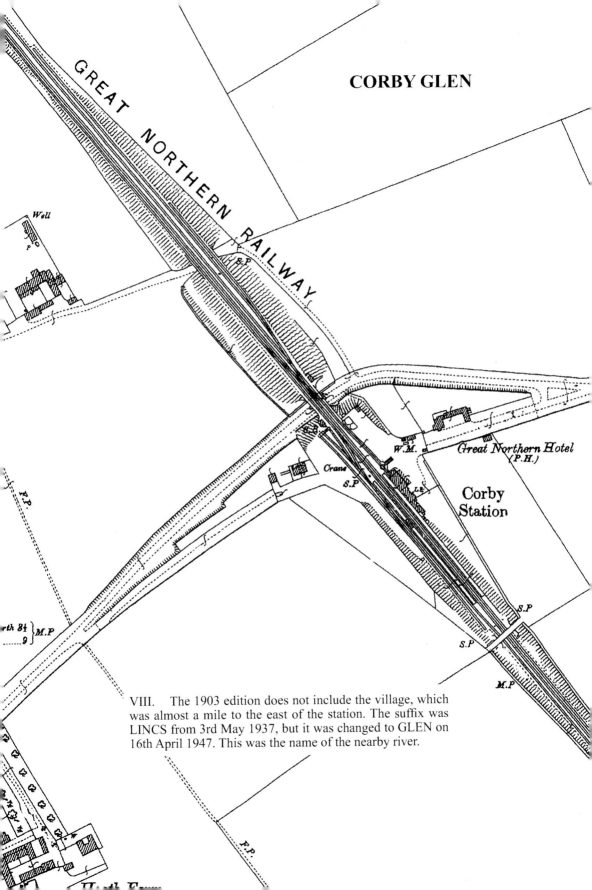

CORBY GLEN

GREAT NORTHERN RAILWAY

Well

Great Northern Hotel
(P.H.)

W.M.

Crane

S.P

Corby
Station

M.P

S.P

S.P

M.P

VIII.   The 1903 edition does not include the village, which was almost a mile to the east of the station. The suffix was LINCS from 3rd May 1937, but it was changed to GLEN on 16th April 1947. This was the name of the nearby river.

58.   As elsewhere, new buildings came with the track quadrupling, but seldom was the GNR's self promotion so evident. While many railways rotated their nameboards slightly, few did so with their lamps. (LOSA)

59.   A northward panorama on 30th June 1956 features class V2 2-6-2 no. 60832, with an up express. The signal box was the third one on the site and its 75-lever frame was in use from 1913 until 27th April 1975. The local population was only 718 in 1901. (J.Chesney)

60.   Class A3 no. 60063 *Isinglass* is approaching on 26th September 1958, with a down stopping train. Trains ceased to call on 15th June 1959. The yard crane was rated at 4 tons 18 cwt. (R.G.Nelson/T.Walsh)

61.   Photographed on the same day is a mixed freight train, hauled by class V2 2-6-2 no. 60914. The goods yard in the background closed on 5th October 1964. (R.G.Nelson/T.Walsh)

NORTH OF CORBY GLEN

62.   Stoke Tunnel is near the summit of the route and is 880 yds in length. Two "Atlantic" class ex-GNR locomotives make a rare combination at the head of a Doncaster Plant Special on 20th September 1953. Nearby was Stoke signal box which had 24 levers, which were operated from 1886 until 6th July 1975. South of it had been the 20-lever Burton box, open 1913-28. (P.J.Garland/R.S.Carpenter)

63.   Seen between the tunnel and the box at Stoke on 26th August 1959 is the up "Northumbrian", devoid of its headboard. The hill top is evident. (P.H.Groom)

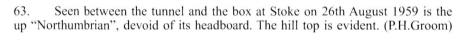

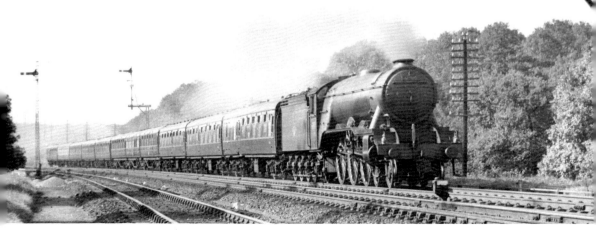

64.   Next on the journey is High Dyke Junction, where an important mineral line branched south. At its west end was Sproxton Quarry which opened in 1925. By the late 1930s, up to 15 trains of iron ore were leaving this junction daily. Class 02 nos 63931 and 63956 are seen on 7th June 1963. (Bentley coll.)

65.   The first mine in the district opened in 1911 and two more followed, but traffic diminished and ceased in 1973. This view south is from July 1964. The box had 40 levers and was in use from 1882 until 24th October 1977. (J.Chesney)

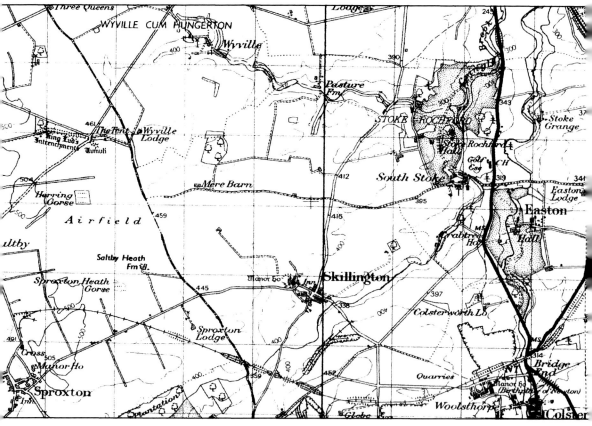

IX.   This extract is at 1 ins to 1 mile and is from the 1952 survey, but not all the quarry lines are shown. The junction illustrated in picture 65 is top right and the line at the lower border continued to a junction on the Saxby - Bourne line. Most quarrying was in the lower part of this map.

66.   This quarry was near Colsterworth and the wagons are on 3ft 6ins track at this location. After removal of the iron ore, the upper ground layers were usually replaced. (A.Dudman coll.)

GREAT PONTON

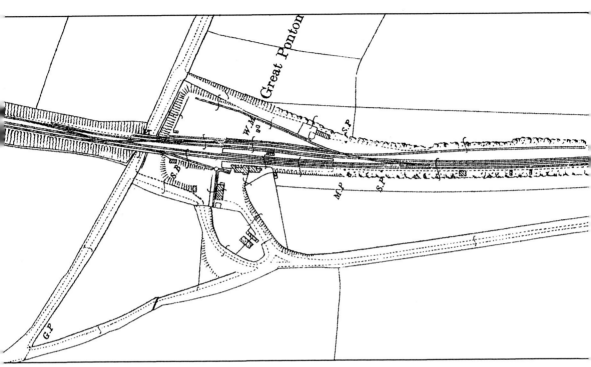

X.   The 1904 edition is at 20 ins to 1 mile. The village housed 400 souls in 1901 and 322 in 1961.

67.   We look south in about 1930 and can enjoy some unusual chimneys. On the left is the up platform, which never had a footbridge for access. (Stations UK)

68.   A K3 class 2-6-0 is seen in about 1947 working "Down perishables", which probably means fish. Such vans were fitted with driver controlled brakes and ran at high speed. The siding has a wagon turntable beyond the crossing. (J.Chesney)

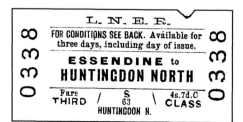

L. N. E. R.

FOR CONDITIONS SEE BACK. Available for three days, including day of issue.

ESSENDINE to
HUNTINGDON NORTH

Fare / S \ 4s.7d.C
THIRD / 63 \ CLASS
HUNTINGDON N.

0338   0338

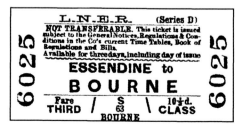

L. N. E. R.   (Series D)

NOT TRANSFERABLE. This ticket is issued subject to the General Notices, Regulations & Conditions in the Co's current Time Tables, Book of Regulations and Bills.
Available for three days, including day of issue

ESSENDINE to
BOURNE

Fare / S \ 10½d.
THIRD / 63 \ CLASS
BOURNE

6025   6025

69.　　Class V2 2-6-2 no. 60870 is working hard with an up freight on 15th October 1955. The 18-lever box of 1874 was replaced by the one seen on 19th July 1942. It lasted until 6th February 1972 and had 30 levers. (J.Chesney)

70.　　There were only two platforms for passengers, but there was one for cattle (right). Passenger service ceased here on 15th September 1958 and goods followed on 29th April 1963. The panorama is from 28th May 1956 and includes the 5-ton crane. (B.W.L.Brooksbank coll.)

NORTH OF GREAT PONTON

71.   No. 90115 was an ex-War Department 2-8-0, one of a large number borrowed by the LNER from the Ministry of Supply and classified WD. There were three or four tracks on the approach to Grantham. There was an intermediate signal box at Saltersford from 1874 to 1932. (P.H.Groom/M.J.Stretton)

SOUTH OF GRANTHAM

72.   No. 55002 *The King's Own Yorkshire Light Infantry* accelerates south, bound for King's Cross on 23rd August 1980. The station is in the background and Aveling-Barford's premises are on the right. The company was formed in February 1934, after merging the country's two best known steam roller producers. Before and since, they have been noted for earth moving equipment. (T.Heavyside)

GRANTHAM

XI.   The ECML is from lower right to top centre on this 1904 edition at 6ins to 1 mile. Lower left is the Grantham Canal, which passes near the Gas Works to terminate at The Wharf. This was the location of the town's first station, with trains coming from Nottingham on the curve top left. The junction signal box was called Barrowby Road and its 35-lever frame was in use until 4th August 1968.

a { Grantham R.D. (Det.)
   { Spittlegate Without Ph. (Det.)
b { Grantham Grange Ph.

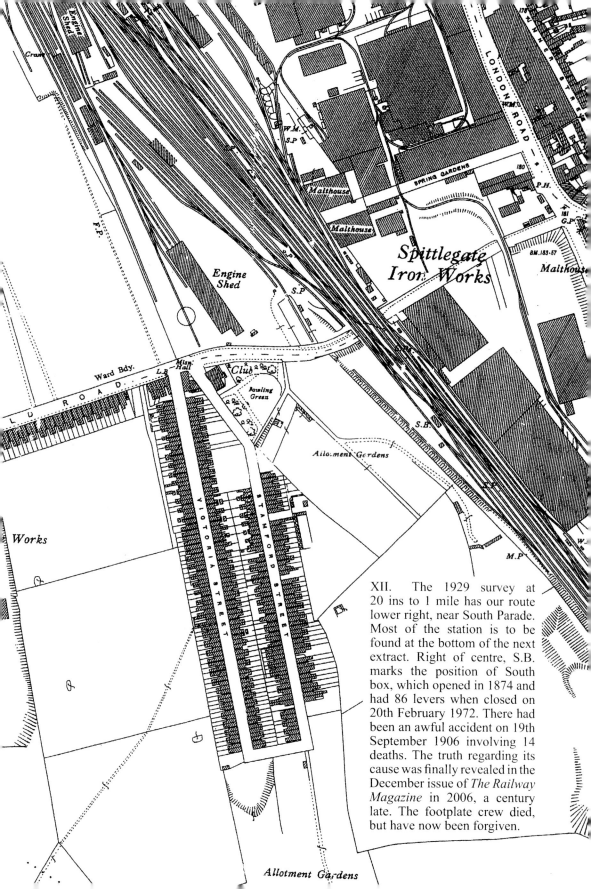

Engine
Shed

Crane

F.P.

Engine
Shed

Malthouse

Malthouse

W.M.
S.P.

LONDON ROAD

SPRING GARDENS

180

P.H.

181
G.P.

BM.183·57

Spittlegate
Iron Works

Malthouse

S.P.

S.P.

Ward Bdy.

L.B.

Misn
Hall

Club

Bowling
Green

ELD ROAD

S.B.

Allotment Gardens

Works

VICTORIA STREET

STAMFORD STREET

M.P.

W.

Allotment Gardens

XII. The 1929 survey at 20 ins to 1 mile has our route lower right, near South Parade. Most of the station is to be found at the bottom of the next extract. Right of centre, S.B. marks the position of South box, which opened in 1874 and had 86 levers when closed on 20th February 1972. There had been an awful accident on 19th September 1906 involving 14 deaths. The truth regarding its cause was finally revealed in the December issue of *The Railway Magazine* in 2006, a century late. The footplate crew died, but have now been forgiven.

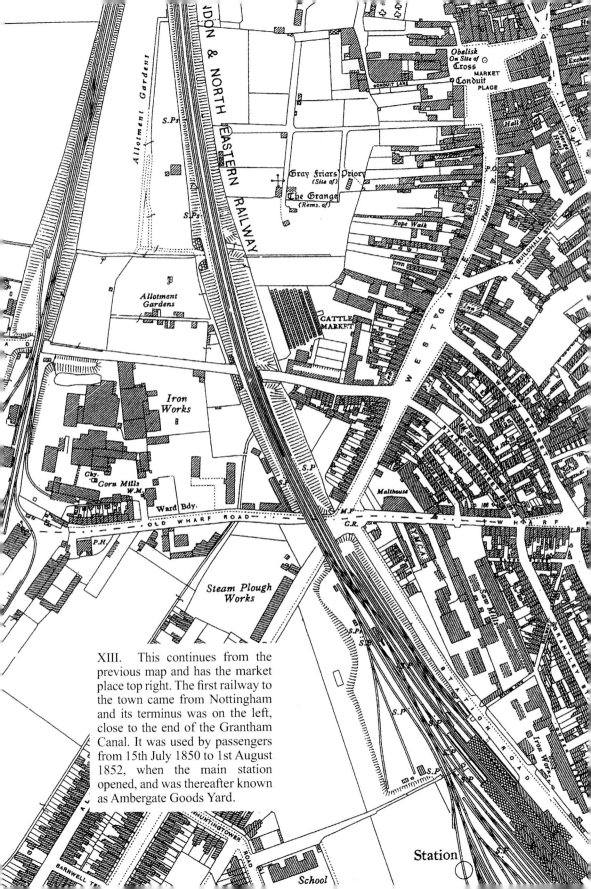

XIII. This continues from the previous map and has the market place top right. The first railway to the town came from Nottingham and its terminus was on the left, close to the end of the Grantham Canal. It was used by passengers from 15th July 1850 to 1st August 1852, when the main station opened, and was thereafter known as Ambergate Goods Yard.

73.　　We are looking south east as a class A4 approaches sometime in 1939. A single milk churn confirms that most milk went by tanker by that time. The two bays were used by local trains, mostly running to branches. The up platform was raised and lengthened in 1945. (Stations UK)

74.　　A train from Newcastle to Kings Cross is seen on 8th July 1948, hauled by class A3 4-6-2 no.77 *The White Knight*, soon to become no. 60077 under BR numbering. Many London passengers had to change here for Sleaford, Lincoln and so on. (H.C.Casserley)

75.	A view south along the up platform includes a poster board headed steamships, plus several of the carriage sidings. The spaced coacting signals ensured that the visual obstruction caused by the footbridge allowed one to be seen. (LOSA)

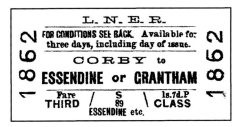

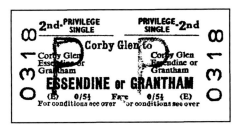

76.   Class A1 4-6-2 no. 60131 *Osprey* is backing onto an express during a locomotive change over in the summer of 1952. The frosted glass in the oval window was for privacy reasons. The finial of Yard Box is above the tender. (P.Kingston)

BRITISH RLYS. ⒸⒹ	BRITISH RLYS. ⒸⒹ
For conditions see back	For conditions see back
Available for three days including day of issue.	Available for three days including day of issue.
Grantham	Grantham
GRANTHAM to	
MANSFIELD (L.N.E.)	
MANSFIELD LNE	MANSFIELD LNE
3rd. 7s.3d.Z	3rd. 7s.3d.Z

2830   2830

L. N. E. R.
FURLOUGH
FOR CONDITIONS SEE BACK. Available for three days, including day of issue.
GRANTHAM to
PETERBORO' NORTH
THIRD   /S.M.Fur.S.\   CLASS
        91
PETERBORO' NORTH

1954   1954

77.   This is the south end in 1952, with the entrance and its many chimneys top left and one of the engine sheds lower left. Yard Box is in the gloom on the right. (Milepost 92½)

78.   North Box is on the right as no. 69809 arrives from the north. It is a class A5 4-6-2T, one of a group of 43 begun in 1911. To the left of the lamp post is a cupboard which contains a stretcher. They were common on stations, as were accidents. No date is available. (Colour-Rail.com)

79.   Yard Box is on the right as class A2/1 no. 60508 *Duke of Rothesay* obstructs the barrow crossing, sometime in 1953. The town had grown from 5762 in 1901 to 25,420 in 1961, largely due to the railway. (R.S.Carpenter)

80.　　Pictured on 8th July 1948 is class D3 4-4-0 no. 2000, which was kept in good condition as it was used for working officers inspection saloons. It had side windows for this reason. (H.C.Casserley)

81.　　Seen on the same day is no. 2810, a class C1 4-4-2 of 1902. Ninety-four were built by the GNR. Above its tender is the coaling tower and on the right is the water tank. The former is the next view point. These facilities were completed in 1938, when 1000 tons of coal was consumed each week by locomotives. (H.C.Casserley)

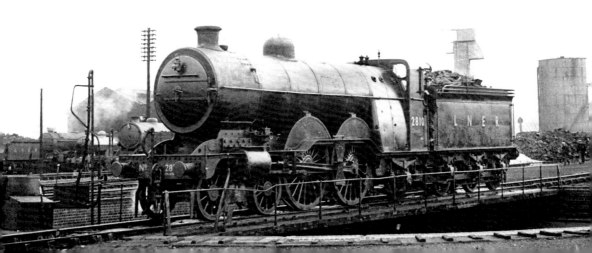

82.   This is a southward panorama in about 1950, with white heaps of ash in profusion.
There was a turntable to the right of the shed and another one further north. They were replaced by
a complex triangular system. (Milepost 92½)

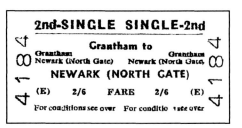

83.   It is 18th May 1959 and class A5/1 4-6-2T no. 69814 waits at platform 5 with a local train. Noted in the shed yard were nos 90059, 60893, 69516 and 60858. (J.Chesney)

84.   This was the younger of the two sheds and was of GNR origin. Ex-WD 2-8-0 no. 90598 is seen on 8th September 1963, shortly before depot closure. Its code was 35B in 1949-58 and 34F to the end. There was an allocation of 41 engines here in 1959; this included 15 named ones. (R.S.Carpenter)

85. This is a northward view of the 1850 terminus serving as Ambergate Goods Yard in 1964. The line ran further south to the gas works, which had originally received its coal by barge. It was supplied by rail until its closure around 1970. (Stations UK)

XIV. Here is a copy of the first timetable for passengers to the town and the company was unusual in having "and" twice in its name. The reference to Greenwich Time meant that there were still local variations throughout the country.

Amber Gate, Nottingham and Boston, and Eastern Junction Railway.

TIME-TABLE FOR JULY, 1850.

GREENWICH TIME IS KEPT AT ALL THE STATIONS.

STATIONS.	DOWN. Nottingham to Grantham.					Sundays.		FARES from Nottingham			
		1	2	3	4	1	2				
	Miles	1st 2nd and 3rd Class	1st 2nd & Gov.	Express	1st 2nd and 3rd Class	1st 2nd & Gov.	1st 2nd and 3rd Class	1st Class s. d.	2nd Class s. d.	3rd Class s. d.	4th Class s. d.
Departure from		a. m.	p. m.	p. m.	p. m.	a. m.	p. m.				
Nottingham	...	10 10	1 15	3 45	9 5	9 0	8 0	...	...	...	...
Ratcliffe	6½	10 25	1 39	3 58	9 20	9 16	8 16	1 6	1 0	0 6	0 5½
Bingham	9	10 37	1 56	4 8	9 33	9 30	8 30	2 3	1 6	0 9	0 9
Aslockton	10½	10 42	2 4	4 13	9 39	9 36	8 36	2 7	1 9	0 11	0 10½
Elton	13	10 49	2 14	4 20	9 47	9 44	8 44	3 3	2 2	1 1	1 1
Bottesford	15½	10 58	2 28	4 29	9 56	9 54	8 54	3 11	2 7	1 4	1 3½
Sedgebrook	18½	11 5	2 43	4 36	10 5	10 4	9 4	4 7	3 1	1 7	1 6½
Grantham	22½	11 15	3 0	4 45	10 15	10 15	9 15	5 0	3 9	1 11	1 10½

STATIONS.	UP. Grantham to Nottingham.					Sundays.		FARES from Grantham.			
		1	2	3	4	1	2				
	Miles	1st 2nd and 3rd Class	1st 2nd & Gov.	Express	1st 2nd and 3rd Class	1st 2nd & Gov.	1st 2nd and 3rd Class	1st Class s. d.	2nd Class s. d.	3rd Class s. d.	4th Class s. d.
Departure from		a. m.	a. m.	p. m.	p. m.	a. m.	p. m.				
Grantham	...	8 40	11 0	2 20	7 0	7 30	6 30	...	...	...	...
Sedgebrook	4½	8 53	11 18	2 30	7 12	7 43	6 43	1 3	1 0	0 6	0 4½
Bottesford	7	9 3	11 34	2 38	7 22	7 53	6 53	1 9	1 2	0 7	0 7
Elton	9½	9 12	11 46	2 46	7 30	8 2	7 2	2 5	1 7	0 10	0 9½
Aslockton	12½	9 20	11 56	2 51	7 38	8 10	7 10	3 0	2 0	1 1	1 0½
Bingham	13½	9 28	12 6	2 57	7 46	8 18	7 18	3 5	2 3	1 2	1 1½
Ratcliffe	17½	9 42	12 24	3 8	7 56	8 32	7 32	4 8	2 11	1 6	1 5½
Nottingham	22½	9 55	12 45	3 20	8 10	8 45	7 45	5 0	3 9	1 11	1 10½

PASSENGERS LUGGAGE.—The Company do not hold themselves responsible for Luggage, unless Booked and paid for according to its value.—100 lbs. weight of Luggage is allowed to First Class, 60 lbs. weight to Second Class, and 40 lbs. weight to Third Class Passengers, not being Merchandise, or any other Articles carried for hire or profit; any excess above that weight will be charged.

☞ The Company do not GUARANTEE the arrival of the Trains at the respective Stations at the times stated, but will use their best endeavours TO ENSURE PUNCTUALITY.

JOHN GOUGH, Secretary.

86.   A class 55 arrives with Pullman cars sometime in 1964. Between the water column and the loco crew is a "Fire Devil". This was a stove which was lit on frosty nights to keep the equipment warm. (Stations UK)

87.   Grantham North box opened in 1881 and its 105 levers fell silent on 20th February 1972. The DMU has probably come from Sheffield in about 1964, after "Cats Whiskers" had been replaced by yellow square panels. (J.Chesney)

88.   It is 2nd May 1975 and no. 47433 is under the footbridge as it runs in with the 14.20 Kings Cross to Leeds. In the bay is the DMU connection for Skegness. It would pass the sites of three signal boxes; Barrowby Road, Peascliffe and Belton. (T.Heavyside)

89.   This box had been called Grantham Yard until 20th February 1972, when the two adjacent boxes closed. The suffix was dropped and its 51-lever frame was replaced by a panel. Its closure came on 3rd February 1980. Near it on 23rd August of that year is no. 55011 *The Royal Northumberland Fusiliers* with the 16.05 Kings Cross to York. The extent of the yard is apparent. (T.Heavyside)

90.   Many large stations employed resident cats to manage vermin and a record was claimed here on 17th September 2000 when "Shag" died after 17 years of service. This and the following three views complete a survey on 6th August 2003. This shelter was known as a port cochère. (A.C.Hartless)

91.   Looking south along platform 4, no. 170399 is seen arriving with the 15.03 Norwich to Liverpool. The up and down goods line is to the right of the train. This platform would take 12 coaches whereas the other two through ones could accommodate 14 by 2006. (A.C.Hartless)

L.N.E.R.
CHILD
FOR CONDITIONS SEE BACK. Available for three days, including day of issue.
GREAT PONTON to
GRANTHAM
Third Class Fare 4½d.C
8809 8809

L.N.E.R.
FOR CONDITIONS SEE BACK. Available for three days, including day of issue.
GREAT PONTON to
GRANTHAM
Fare S 5½d.N
THIRD 90 CLASS
GRANTHAM
8092 8092

92.   The 14.00 Edinburgh - Kings Cross hurries southward through platform 1. Platforms 2 - 4 are an island, accessible only by the footbridge. Platform 1 has ex-GNR buildings with a modern replacement canopy. The refurbishment took place in 1986 and many new stanchions of the old style were cast. Passenger lifts arrived in 2007. (A.C.Hartless)

93.   No. 156408 arrived in the down bay on time with the 14.44 Blythe Bridge to Skegness, but was failed with low coolant level. This cross country service normally originated from Manchester Airport, but was curtailed because of resignalling and trackwork at Stoke-on-Trent. (A.C.Hartless)

NORTH OF GRANTHAM

94.   A branch was built in 1914-15 by Sir John Jackson Ltd to create the Belton Park Military Railway. It served the Machine Gun Corps, which had been formed on 14th October 1915. A WD locomotive ran to and from a Grantham yard, twice a day on most occasions. (Unknown)

XV.   Diagram of the BPMR indicates its relationship to the ECML, where the junction was controlled by Belton signal box (1882-1922). The depot shut in 1919 and the branch closed in 1921.

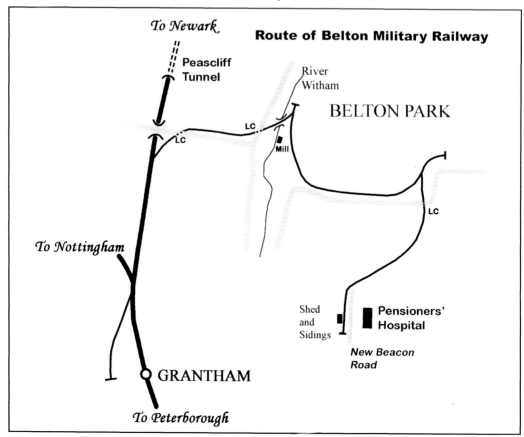

BARKSTON

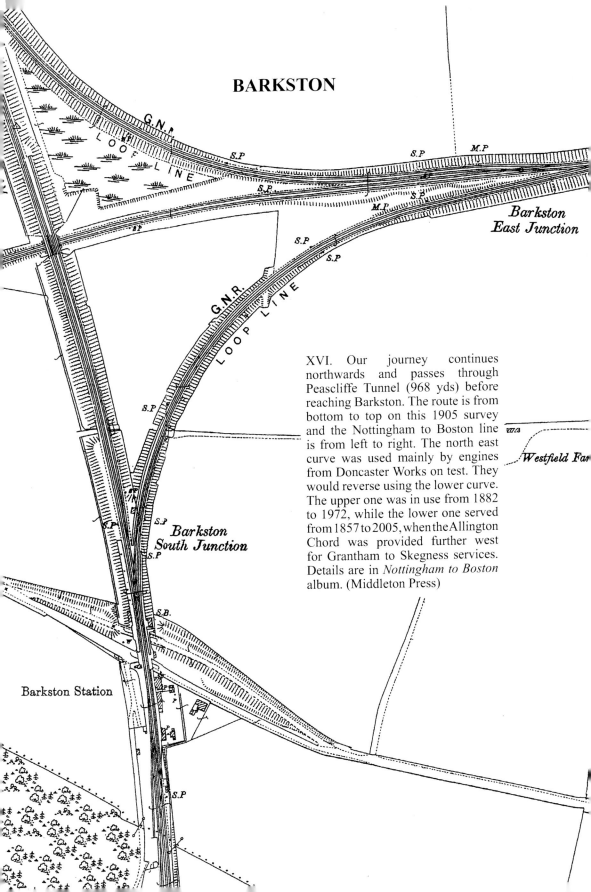

G.N.R. LOOF LINE

S.P.   S.P.   M.P.

Barkston
East Junction

G.N.R. LOOP LINE

S.P.

S.P.

M.P.

S.P.

S.P.

S.P.

Westfield Far

S.P.

S.P.

Barkston
South Junction

S.P.

S.B.

Barkston Station

S.P.

XVI. Our journey continues northwards and passes through Peascliffe Tunnel (968 yds) before reaching Barkston. The route is from bottom to top on this 1905 survey and the Nottingham to Boston line is from left to right. The north east curve was used mainly by engines from Doncaster Works on test. They would reverse using the lower curve. The upper one was in use from 1882 to 1972, while the lower one served from 1857 to 2005, when the Allington Chord was provided further west for Grantham to Skegness services. Details are in *Nottingham to Boston* album. (Middleton Press)

95. South Box and the main buildings are shown lower left on the map. In the foreground is part of the short siding. It remained open until 6th July 1964, but passenger service ceased on 16th March 1955. (LOSA)

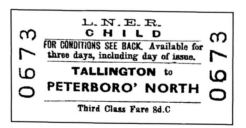

96.   The same buildings are seen from the north in about 1939. The structures lower left are part of the bridge over the road. The name was Barkstone until 1916. (Stations UK)

97.   We look north in the same era and find that there was a third platform and a second siding, this being for cripple purposes as there was no access to it. (Stations UK)

98.   South Junction Box remained to be photographed on 7th June 1963, it having been built in 1876. It had a 35-lever frame and was worked until 30th April 1972. Passing is no. 61367, a class B1 4-6-0 of LNER origin. The hut near the doorway contained a toilet. North Box had 20 levers and closed on the same day. (Bentley coll.)

99.   Only the name remained to be photographed on 23rd August 1980. A Bridlington to Kings Cross train passes, hauled by no. 40117. This was one of the many extra trains run for holiday makers each summer. (T.Heavyside)

HOUGHAM

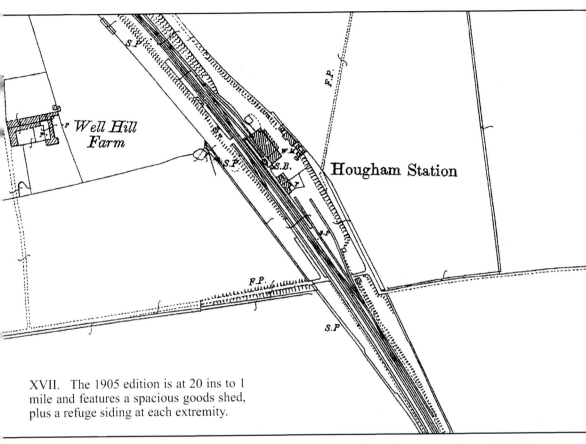

XVII. The 1905 edition is at 20 ins to 1 mile and features a spacious goods shed, plus a refuge siding at each extremity.

100. The staggering of the platforms is evident in this southward panorama from 28th May 1956. The village housed 200 in 1901 and 117 in 1961 and so few could demand a footbridge. (B.W.L.Brooksbank)

101.   Pictured on 6th August 1959 is class A1 4-6-2 no. 60144 *King's Courier*. Both passenger and goods services had been withdrawn here on 16th September 1957. The next box northwards was Westborough and it had just six levers, closing on 14th June 1964. The trolley is on wooden rails. (J.Chesney)

102.   The remains are seen in 1960, looking northwards. The 1891 signal box had 30 levers and closed on 30th April 1972. The station had the suffix "& Marston" until 1856. (B.W.L.Brooksbank)

CLAYPOLE

XVIII. The 1914 edition includes refuge sidings,
up and down. They were needed with so many
expresses on the route. An up electrified loop was
later provided here and a down one was created
further north. They had opened in 1938-41.

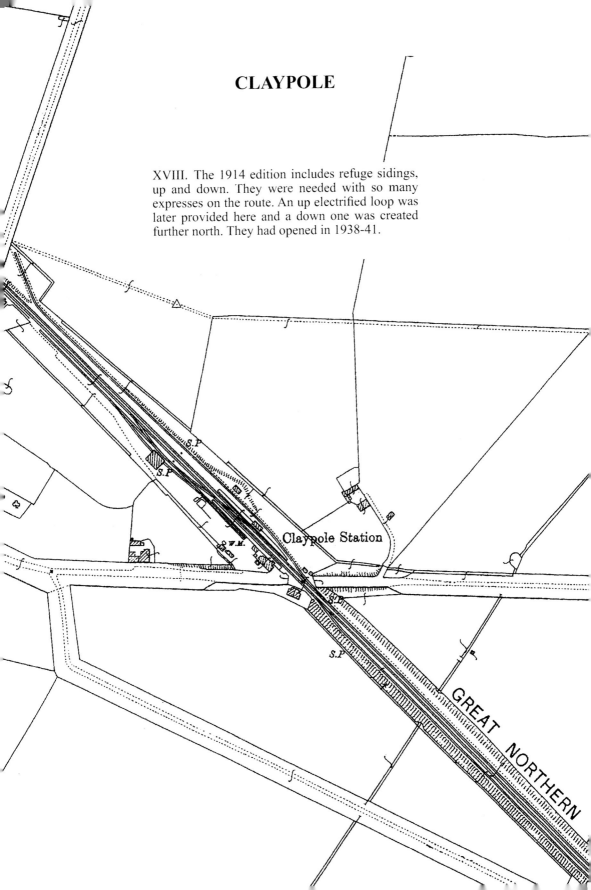

Claypole Station

GREAT NORTHERN

103.	A damaged postcard shows the view towards Newark in about 1900. Standing on the up refuge siding is class C2 4-4-2 no. 987. (LOSA)

104.	Another card from the same maker and this features the 1875 35-lever box, which was in use until 11th July 1977. It was replaced by a flat roofed structure containing a panel. It became a gate box on 3rd February 1980 and was still in use in 2014. (LOSA)

105.   Two views from 1954 complete the survey, the station closing to passengers on 16th September 1957. The goods yard remained in use until 6th July 1964, but it did not have a crane. (Stations UK)

106.   A view southeast shows the convenient procedure of hanging fire buckets on the convenience for gentlemen; the tap was nearby. There were 542 residents in 1901, this rising to 724 in 1961. (Stations UK)

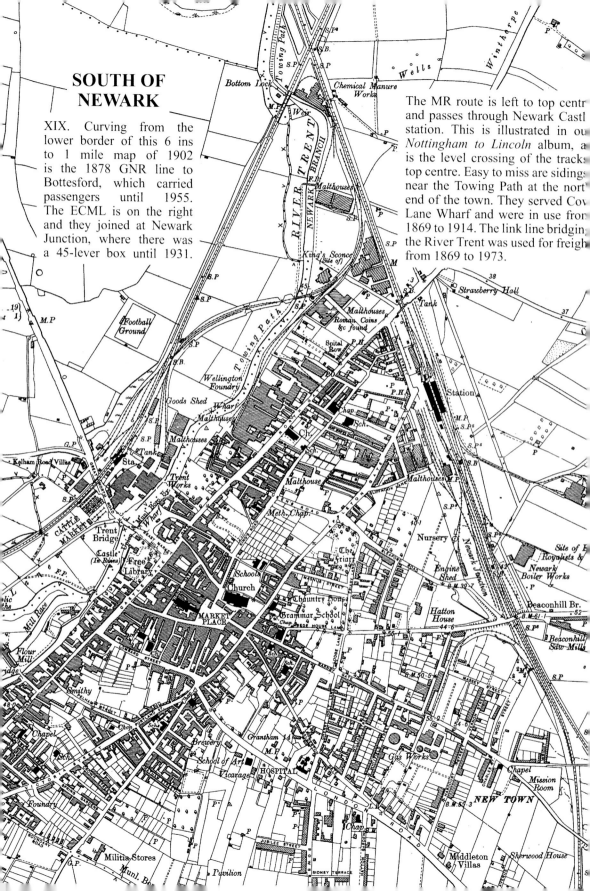

SOUTH OF NEWARK

XIX. Curving from the lower border of this 6 ins to 1 mile map of 1902 is the 1878 GNR line to Bottesford, which carried passengers until 1955. The ECML is on the right and they joined at Newark Junction, where there was a 45-lever box until 1931.

The MR route is left to top centr and passes through Newark Castl station. This is illustrated in ou *Nottingham to Lincoln* album, a is the level crossing of the track top centre. Easy to miss are siding near the Towing Path at the nort end of the town. They served Cov Lane Wharf and were in use fro 1869 to 1914. The link line bridgin the River Trent was used for freigh from 1869 to 1973.

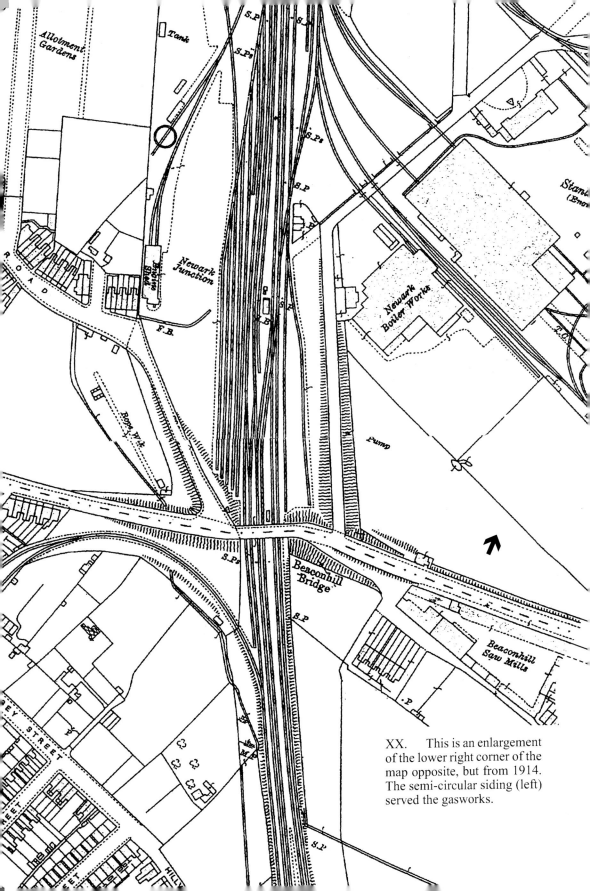

Allotment Gardens

Tank

S.P.

S.Ps

S.Ps

ROAD

Newark Junction

F.B.

Boro' Wks

S.P.

S.Ps

Newark Boiler Works

Stan (Eno)

Pump

Beaconhill Bridge

S.P.

Beaconhill Saw Mills

STREET

M.P.

XX.   This is an enlargement of the lower right corner of the map opposite, but from 1914. The semi-circular siding (left) served the gasworks.

S.P.

107.   The engine shed came into use in 1880 and housed four locos. It is seen on 14th April 1958, with no. 58065, a class 1P 0-4-4T. This type was made by the MR from 1881 onwards. Class J6 0-6-0 no. 64234 is on the left. (P.H.Groom)

108.   The shed closed on 5th January 1959. A snap from 17th August 1958 features no. 64236, a class J6 0-6-0. The LNWR had run a Northampton to Scarborough service via Bottesford for some years, but locomotives were always changed here. (R.S.Carpenter)

NEWARK NORTHGATE

109.   A postcard view north has a footbridge in the distance which was near a road called "North Gate". This was part of the Roman Road named "Fosse Way". The white block on the right was a stepping stone for staff crossing the track. (P.Laming coll.)

110.   Another splendid postcard and this includes recessed footholds, plus well presented staff and gas lamps. The Lamp Room and the Porters Room are on the left. (P.Laming coll.)

XXI.   The 1914 edition has been enlarged to 35 ins to 1 mile and shows that two malthouses had wagon turntables. These sidings were completed in 1881.

Allotment   Garde

Tanks

S.B.

S.P.

Goods Shed

NORTH GATE

LINCOLN   STREET

STREET

ALLIANCE

Allotment
Gardens

Railway Hotel
(P.H.)

Malthouses

Roman Coins &
found

Allotment
Gardens

P.H.

SUMMER'S ROAD

Tinker
Yard

d Row

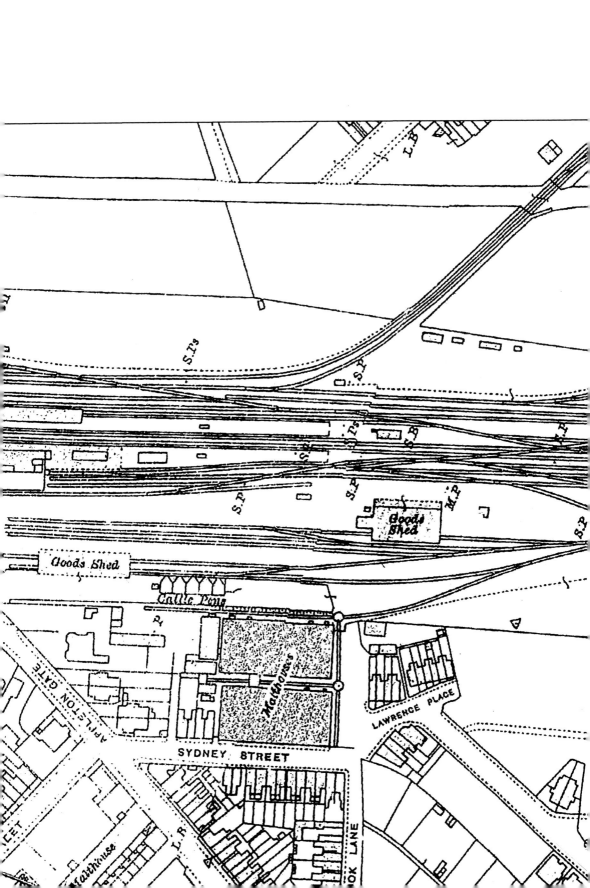

Abbott & Co.'s Siding......	L. N. E. (G. N.)	Newark.
Baird, Hugh, & Sons, Ltd.—		
Cliff Nook Kilns	L. N. E. (G. N.)	Newark.
Concrete Kilns, Nos. 2 & 3	L.M.S. (Mid.)	Newark.
Spital Kiln No. 1	LNE & LMSJt.(GN&Mid.)	Joint Curve.
Bishop & Son—		
Cow Lane Malt Kiln	LNE&LMSJt. (GN&Mid.)	Joint Curve.
Spital Maltings	LNE&LMSJt.(GN&Mid.)	Joint Curve.
Branston's—		
Maltings (L. N. E.)	L.N.E. (GN)–LMS. (Mid.)	Newark.
Riverside Malt Kiln	LNE & LMSJt.(GN&Mid.)	Joint Curve.
British Glues & Chemicals, Ltd., Siding (L. N. E.)	{ L. N. E. (G. N.)–L. M. S. (Mid.)	Newark.
British Sugar Corporation, Ltd., Kelham Siding	L. M. S. (Mid.)	Newark.
Cafferata & Co.—		
Bowbridge Siding........	L. N. E. (G. N.)	Newark and Cotham.
Jericho Siding..............	L. N. E. (G. N.)	Newark and Bottesford.
Siding	L. N. E. (G. N.)	Newark.
Cross Street Siding	L. N. E. (G. N.)	Newark and Cotham.
Farrar's Siding	LNE & LMSJt.(GN&Mid.)	Joint Curve.
Gilstrap, Earp & Co.—		
Cow Lane Maltings......	LNE & LMSJt.(GN&Mid.)	Joint Curve.
Maltings (L. N. E.)	L.N.E. (G.N.)–LMS (Mid.)	Newark.
Massey Sidings	LNE & LMSJt.(GN&Mid.)	Joint Curve.
Grain Yard (L. N. E.)........	L. N. E. (G.N.)–L. M. S. (L. N. W.)	Same as Newark (L. N. E.) Goods
Kerol, Ltd.	L. N. E. (G. N.)	British Glues & Chemicals, Ltd., Sid.
Lowfield Sidings..............	L. N. E. (G. N.)	Newark and Cotham.
Muskham Siding	L. N. E. (G. N.)	Newark and Carlton-on-Trent.
Newark Gas Co.'s Siding (Cross Street)	L. N. E. (G. N.)	Newark and Cotham.
Newark Gravel & Concrete Co.'s Siding, Balderton...	L. N. E. (G. N.)............	Newark and Bottesford.
Parnham & Son's Water Mill (L. M. S.)................	L.M.S. (Mid.)–L.N.E.(GN)	Nottingham and Newark.
Pure Bone Phosphate Co., Ltd.	L. N. E. (G. N.)	Cafferata & Co.'s Siding.
Ransome & Co.'s Siding...	L. N. E. (G. N.)	Newark.
Ransome & Marles Bearing Co., Ltd.	L. N. E. (G. N.)	Newark.
Ruston & Hornsby, Ltd., Iron Works	LNE & LMS Jt.(GN&Mid)	Joint Curve.
Trent Concrete Co............	{ L. N. E. & L. M. S. Jt. (G. N. & Mid.)........	Bishop & Son's Cow Lane Malt Kiln.
Ward, T. W., Ltd............	L. N. E. (G. N.)............	Lowfield Sidings.
Warwick & Richardson's Sid	LNE & LMS Jt.(GN&Mid)	Joint Curve.
Worthington Simpsons, Ltd., Siding	L. N. E. (G. N.)	Lowfield Sidings.
Newark Gas Co.'s Siding......	L. N. E. (G. N.)	Newark.
Newark Gravel & Concrete Co.'s Siding, Balderton......	L. N. E. (G. N.)	Newark.

XXII.   The 1938 Railway Clearing House Hand Book data on the sidings listed, plus the route from which they diverged and their sites.

111.   A 1953 trio of pictures are all looking south. In this one we can enjoy the delicate tracery on the stanchions, as the sunlight is so low. (Stations UK)

112.   The up bay platform had excellent weather protection, which was of particular value during heavy mailbag traffic. The arches can be seen in the background of the previous picture. (Stations UK)

113.   An express from London offers a clear exhaust as the photographer waits on the footbridge and we marvel at the fenestrated chimneys; pity about the odd pots though. It is unusual that parts of the canopies needed extra support. (Milepost 92½)

114.   The suffix "North Gate" was issued on 25th September 1950, but it was soon appearing as one word, as shown in this 1964 northward panorama. Both have been used subsequently. The covered bay is on the right and part of the down yard is on the left. (Stations UK)

115.   No. 47459 is slowing down as it arrives with the 08.53 Bradford to King's Cross express, on 9th October 1976. Minimal shelter must have reduced passenger numbers. (T.Heavyside)

116.　　No. 47546 departs on 30th April 1977 hauling a Newcastle to King's Cross train formed of mostly Mk.II coaches. The three-storey goods shed is behind it. (J.Whitehouse)

117.　　No. 47410 is working a Hull to King's Cross train on the same day and South Box comes into view. It was in use from 1931 until 3rd February 1980 and had 105 levers. The DMU bears the name "Cleethorpes" and is on the reversing siding. (J.Whitehouse)

118.　The west elevation was recorded on 26th October 1979. This important town of Newark grew from 15,159 in 1901 to 24,670 in 1961. The down platform was fit for 12 coaches. (D.A.Thompson)

119.　The down side was photographed on the same day. An east to south curve was completed north of the station in 1965, which allowed Lincoln trains to use this station. The bay platform was eliminated and a reversible loop for 15 coaches provided at platform 3. Nearby were five sidings, the western one being electrified later. (D.A.Thompson)

120. A Grand Central train speeds through on 8th June 2013, bound for Sunderland. Their HSTs were unusual in having buffers. Fitted with a pair of lifts, the new footbridge enhanced the facilities from 2007 onwards. (P. Jones)

For other views of this station, see our album *Newark to Doncaster.*

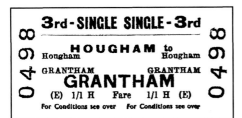

MP Middleton Press
EVOLVING THE ULTIMATE RAIL ENCYCLOPEDIA

Easebourne Midhurst GU29 9AZ. Tel:01730 813169

www.middletonpress.co.uk email:info@middletonpress.co.uk
A-978 0 906520 B- 978 1 873793 C- 978 1 901706 D-978 1 904474
E - 978 1 906008 F - 978 1 908174